GREEK HORIZONS

Helen Hill Miller

GREEK
HORIZONS

New York

CHARLES SCRIBNER'S SONS

Grateful acknowledgment is made for permission to quote the following exerpts: p. 90 Euripides: *Medea* tr. Gilbert Murray, GEORGE ALLEN & UNWIN LTD., London and OXFORD UNIVERSITY PRESS, New York; p. 18 Geoffrey Grigson: *The Glory of an Isle of Greece,* AMERICAN HORIZON, INC., New York; p. 128 ff. Troezen Tablet tr. Michael H. Jameson, *Hesperia,* Journal of the American School of Classical Studies, Athens, vol. xxix, No. 2; pp. 136, 141, 153, 213 *Odes of Pindar* tr. Richmond Lattimore, and pp. 89, 175 f. *Complete Greek Tragedies* tr. Richmond Lattimore, THE UNIVERSITY OF CHICAGO PRESS, Chicago; pp. 28, 52, 56 ff. Alfred Zimmern: *The Greek Commonwealth,* p. 182 Stanley Casson: *Ancient Greece,* p. 52 Denys Page: *Sappho and Alcaeus,* THE CLARENDON PRESS, Oxford; pp. 14, 98, 100, 131, 190, 209 *The Greek Anthology* vol. II tr. W. R. Paton, HARVARD UNIVERSITY PRESS, Cambridge; p. 101 ff. Hesiod: *Works and Days* tr. Richmond Lattimore, THE UNIVERSITY OF MICHIGAN PRESS, Ann Arbor; p. 33 ff., 40, 174 Homer: *The Iliad* tr. E. V. Rieu, PENGUIN BOOKS LTD., Harmondsworth, Middlesex; pp. 87 f., 90 *The Complete Greek Drama* tr. Whitney J. Oates & Eugene O'Neill Jr., RANDOM HOUSE, INC., New York

CONTENTS

v

Contents

GREEK HORIZONS

CHAPTER 1 *Arrival in Antiquity*

FOR a first look, the bird's-eye view is best. Foresight can turn arrival into orientation. The dull way to arrive in antiquity is simply to follow the pedestrian logic of logistics, and come straight in from one's prior stopping place. Prudent counsels of time and money recommend it. But two routes provide an initial overview of Greece that is based on loftier logic.

One sweeps across the course of recorded history, east to west, from Asia to Italy: one sees all Greece from the air on a morning flight from Istanbul to Rome.

One follows the traces of prehistory, north to south on an afternoon flight from Vienna to Athens: you traverse the long valleys through which successive mysterious peoples migrated to the islanded peninsula surrounded by the southern sea.

9

Without touching down anywhere, and with millennia foreshortened to minutes, the east-west flight arcs over a panorama whose periphery is that of the Greek world—the cities of Asia Minor, the Aegean islands, the mainland, the Adriatic islands, the colonies of Magna Graecia in Italy, Sicily, and at the delta of the Rhone.

Take-off is from the city by the Golden Horn and the Bosporus, founded about 657 B.C. by Byzas, leader of a colony from Megara, the city-state west of Athens by the Isthmus of Corinth. As Byzantium, it was in existence for close to nine hundred years before it was renamed for the Roman Emperor who established his capital there; as Constantinople, it continued for close to sixteen hundred further years before, in our own time, its name was again changed to Istanbul. (No one is quite sure, incidentally, whether Istanbul is a corruption of the Arabic *Islampol*—"full of Mohammedans"—or the Greek *eis ten polin*—"into the city.")

Behind one, as the plane rises, is the Hellespont. Through its waters the legendary Leander swam to his Hero; across its waters the historic Xerxes of Persia, on bridges cabled with Phoenician flax and papyrus, drove armies numbered by the tens of thousands on the expedition to conquer Greece that was slowed on land at Thermopylae and stopped at sea in the bay of Salamis.

The plane's shadow moves flatly over the tawny waters of the Marmora Sea, then contracts and elongates, rising and falling over the tawny bareness of the Asia Minor hills.

There below was Troy, coast where the hosts of Agamemnon and Achilles camped beside their dark-hulled ships, plain where the Homeric heroes drove swift chariots and clashed sword on shield, citadel of Priam, Hector, and Paris, palace on whose walls Helen watched and the Trojan women wept.

Offshore is the island where the Lesbian Sappho sang of love and where Terpander strung the first full-octaved lyre; below it the island

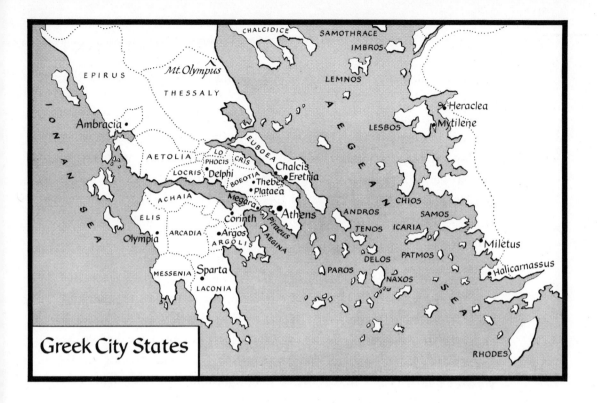

Greek City States

Chios, one among many claimants to be the birthplace of Homer.

Southward across the peninsula were the great Greek cities, Pergamon, with its colossal altar of Zeus; Ephesus, where Oriental splendor invested the cult of the many-breasted Diana; Sardis, capital of Lydia before Cyrus conquered Croesus; Miletus, pre-eminent center of learning—mathematics, astronomy, geography, metaphysics—in the seventh and sixth centuries before the Persian conquest overlaid the spirit of free inquiry; Halicarnassus, Knidus, Xanthus, and many more.

The plane angles west, over purple Aegean waters so thickly islanded from mainland to mainland that even at sea level the crossing is never out of sight of land. At 18,000 feet, the great island groups, with thin white lines of surf along their windward margins, can be successively enumerated: closest to Asia Minor, the Southern Sporades and the Dodecanese, ending with Rhodes; at midpassage, the central Cyclades;

off the Greek mainland, the Northern Sporades and Euboia and the inshore islands on the Saronic Gulf.

As though the steep walls of the Corinth Canal projected up through air space, the plane crosses Greece exactly in its channel. The right-hand windows frame a downward look at Athens and its port, the Peiraeus; the left-hand ones display Corinth and Acrocorinth in the near view, and beyond, the plain of Argos—at this height the forbidding mountains of the Northern Peloponnese are dwarfed by altitude until no barrier remains.

West with the Gulf of Corinth, past the inlet to the north, leading to the massif of Mount Parnassus, that was once used by voyagers consulting the Delphic oracle, the aircraft's course crosses into the Adriatic above the Ionian islands—over Ithaca, where Penelope wove, raveled, and waited; south of Kerkyra, the Corinthian colony later known as Corfu; still farther south of the islands of the Dalmatian coast; north of Kephalonia, center of Odysseus' kingdom, and Zante, ancient way-station for Greek commerce and colonization in the west.

Ahead is the boot of Italy, with cities and towns that were once Greek colonies and are inhabited today, like Naples (near the ancient Cumae), Sybaris, and Tarentum; remains of great centers which last on in imposing ruins, like the temple at Paestum; and legendary obliterated places, like Croton of the great athletes, known today only through stories, shards, and coins.

Fog screens the sea. To the northwest, up the spine of Italy, thunder formations thousands of feet higher than the flight roil and billow in lightning-perforated blacks and grays.

To the southwest, gray-white mist swirls around Sicily; suddenly, detached as in a Japanese print, with fog beneath, around, above it, the black cone of Aetna shows. Below it were Naxos and Syracuse, Gela and Zancle, centers for Greek contact with colonies on the surrounding mainlands—Cyrene in North Africa, Saguntum on the Spanish peninsula, Marseilles at the mouth of the Rhone. Between Sicily and Italy the straits flow between Scylla and Charybdis, the rock and the whirlpool.

The plane dawdles into sunshine west of Capri; the storm moves up the peninsula so fast that soon the landing field at Ciampino is brightly, wetly clear. A right turn, a long descent, a touching down—and the scattered geography of Greek city-states just traversed turns into the consolidated territory of a far-flung empire in which all roads lead to Rome.

The other significant way into antiquity follows the paths along which came the northern migrants who settled Greece before the opening of the period of classical history; paths which successive waves of barbarian raiders used again at its close.

Below the Austrian Alps, the valleys run in north-south parallels, separated by rugged ranges, all the way to the sea. On an afternoon flight from Vienna to the Peiraeus, these narrow channels of pre-historic arrivals are readily clear.

So is their divisiveness, particularly when, below the Greek border, the north-south parallels are crossed by transverse ranges, running east and west, which turn them into a grid.

The grid is the topographic basis for the separateness of the Greek city-states. The inhabitants of each little hollow could and did lead a close-knit existence to themselves alone.

Preferably, their territory included a detached, steep-sided rock, for defense and veneration of the gods; a plain and civic center for ordinary living—agriculture, commerce, and government; a nearby port for access to the sea. Beyond, everything was foreign. In somewhat comparable topography, the Swiss have a word—*kantönlichgeist*—to describe the pocket-preoccupation of their settlements which mountains both isolate and protect.

13

The Greek achievements of antiquity, their innovating and individualized accomplishments in thought, government, architecture, and the creative arts, were based on effective possession of small separate areas of manageable size. Differentiation became possible there as it was impossible in the inchoate contemporary mass-monarchies of the Mediterranean's Asia Minor shores, where the Greek settlements were early debased by autocratic splendor.

But the Greeks were in turn possessed by their boundaries. Their inability to connect their city-states in any wider set of institutions makes of classical history a kaleidoscope in which ephemeral leagues, patterned from minute, brilliant, separate components, succeed each other in ever-altering arrangements as the years turn.

The record is one of connivance and courage, colonization and annihilation, adroitness and treachery, a changeless changing of sides.

Yet when divisiveness was superseded by a temporary and eleventh-hour unity in face of Persian threats under Darius and Xerxes, it was rewarded by the epic sequence of the victory at Marathon, the pass held at Thermopylae, the sea battle at Salamis, the land action at Plataeia.

Simonides' epigrams of celebration show that during this interval, Greece was for all its components a concept with substantial meaning:

"Since the sea parted Europe from Asia, since fierce Ares directs the battles of nations, never was a more splendid deed of arms performed by mortals on land and on the sea at once. For these men after slaying many Medes in Cyprus took a hundred Phoenician ships at sea with their crews. Asia groaned aloud, smitten with both hands by their triumphant might."

"If to die well be the chief part of virtue, Fortune granted this to us above all others; for striving to endue Hellas with freedom, we lie here possessed of praise that groweth not old."

Arrival in Antiquity

"We lie here, having given our lives to save all Hellas when she stood on a razor's edge."

These are things to think on, as the grids merge in rising dusk. Salonika was in shadowed sight below the plains of Thrace at the Aegean's edge. Only minutes later, over Thessaly, a gray veil shrouded Mount Olympus—but are the gods really dead? Darkness obliterates Thermopylae and Marathon.

But darkness becomes Athens. By night, the hastily-built modern suburbs show only as intricate, pin-pointed patterns of light over the whole Attic plain—city, seaport, airfield.

On the ground, the drive to the city's center skirts the base of the dark cliff on whose height is the illuminated Acropolis, separate from all else in beauty and in space.

CHAPTER 2 *The Imminence of Discovery*

THE sites of Greek classical antiquity began to attract Western European visitors at the end of the seventeenth century: Jacques Carrey made detailed drawings of the Acropolis in 1674, and Jacob Spon of France and George Wheeler of Britain toured together in 1675–1676 and published separate impressions a few years later.

In the mid-eighteenth century Johann Joachim Winckelmann of Brandenburg began to assemble a history of Greek art.

By the early nineteenth century, French, German, and English Romantics—Chateaubriand, Victor Hugo, Baudelaire, Goethe, Byron—were busily recording their visits to the ruins of the ancient world.

They wrote much about scenery. The handsome engraved plates that adorn their tooled leather travel books bear such captions as: The Grove at Olympia; the Pass at Thermopylae; the Vale at Delphi.

Byron, in *Childe Harold*, apostrophizes:

> *And yet how lovely in thine age of woe,*
> *Land of lost gods and godlike men, art thou!*
> *Thy vales of evergreens, thy hills of snow,*
> *Proclaim thee Nature's varied favorite now;*
> *Thy fanes, thy temples to thy surface bow,*
> *Commingling slowly with heroic earth,*
> *Broke by the share of every rustic plough:*
> *So perish monuments of mortal birth,*
> *So perish all in turn, save well-recorded Worth.*

They wrote about scenery because in most places scenery was all there was to see. By the time that Byron arrived to join the Greek struggle for independence and die at Missolonghi in 1824, Greece had endured nearly five hundred years of Turkish rule, with power centered in Constantinople and held locally by pashas who served as regional governors. Athens, which had not ranked even as a regional capital, was a minor market town, clustered around the northern base of the Acropolis.

The heights of the Acropolis were reserved for the Turkish administration, which over the years turned the Erechtheion into a harem and the Parthenon first into a mosque with a minaret on the southwest corner and then into a powder magazine—it was a Venetian shell, lobbed during the siege of Athens in 1687, that set off the explosion that destroyed the central part of the structure.

So in the early nineteenth century the temple to Hephaistos, on a rise to the northwest of the Acropolis, was the only classical building relatively intact in the area.

The removal of art treasures from the country, which had begun in Roman times, was still going on; the gentlemen amateurs who practiced archaeology in the late eighteenth and early nineteenth centuries resembled big game hunters in that they took the heads home with them.

Lord Elgin, British Ambassador to the Sublime Porte at the turn of the century, obtained from the Sultan authorizations to catalogue the ruins of the Acropolis and later to remove certain blocks; that is why a number of metopes from the Parthenon, the parts of its frieze depicting the Panathenaic procession, figures from the east and west pediments, and one of the statues of maidens that support the porch of the Erechtheion, are now on view under the name of "the Elgin Marbles" in the British Museum.

Similarly, in 1821, the French Ambassador to Constantinople obtained the Venus de Milo for a gift to his sovereign, Louis XVIII; some forty years later, the Winged Victory of Samothrace alighted in the Louvre.

In 1811, as the vessel bearing the last shipment of "Elgin Marbles" sailed away from the Peiraeus with Lord Byron as a passenger, it passed an open boat. In it were two Germans and two Englishmen, Romantics all, en route the nearby island of Aegina. There, under a crop of barley and less than three feet of soil, they unearthed the archaic figures from the temple of Aphaia. Prince Ludwig of Bavaria promptly bought them to become the showpieces of his new Glyptothek in Munich's Königsplatz.

The diary of one of the English explorers tells how, during their second day's digging, "one of the excavators working in the interior portico, struck on a piece of Parian marble which, as the building itself is of stone (i.e. limestone), arrested his attention. It turned out to be the head of a helmeted warrior, perfect in every feature. It lay with the face turned upwards, and as the features came out by degrees you can imagine nothing like the state of rapture and excitement to which we were wrought."

And while man despoiled the heights, nature was at work in the valleys. Throughout Greece, at the time that the country regained nationhood, almost the sole visible monuments were those on acropolis or headland. Everything that was low enough to be buried by the ceaseless erosion of surrounding hills, or the periodic flooding of swollen rivers, was deep under centuries of silt.

It is only within the past hundred years, and in many cases within the present century, with the speedy development of archaeology as a science, that most of the major Greek sites of the prehistoric and the classical world have once more seen the light.

During the 1870's, work was begun at Troy, Mycenae, and Tiryns among early sites, Delos, Olympia and the Kerameikos Cemetery at Athens among classical ones. In the 1880's, Epidauros, Eleusis, and the Athenian Acropolis began to be cleared. At the turn of the century, Corinth, Aegina, Knossos, Phaistos, and Rhodes were uncovered, and large-scale operations succeeded earlier probes at Delphi. The Athenian Agora has been cleared and one of its stoas restored during the present generation. Archaeologists from practically all countries in the Western world have participated in this revelation of the Western heritage.

The chief centers of the ancient world have thus become visible again only in the time of men still living. Indeed, in what they see, current travelers have more in common with Roman tourists and commentators of the time of the Empire than with those of any later date. The accounts left by Plutarch, Pausanias, and Strabo, of journeys in a Greek world from which power had departed and in which destruction had been great, but a world in which the monuments of the past were still identifiable, still above ground, are a record they can follow.

Pausanias' *Description of Greece*, whose geography Sir James G.

Frazer of Cambridge mapped and verified during the last years of the nineteenth century, is an inventory taken in the middle of the second century A.D. which until the appearance of Baedeker had no rival in meticulous thoroughness. Himself probably a Lydian from Asia Minor, perhaps born at Magnesia, Pausanias lived and traveled during the reign of Marcus Aurelius; he was an immediate successor of Plutarch, a contemporary of Lucian; systematically, over a period that may have extended for forty years, he traversed the Greek countryside, cataloguing the monuments, the religious festivals (except the Eleusinian mysteries, whose secrets he kept because he was an initiate), the legends, the genealogies, the superstitions. He even had his own equivalent of the starred notations of his successors, flagging items for attention with: "This is worth seeing."

If one goes to Olympia, Pausanias can people with precise descriptions the area in which were erected statues of winners of the Games. At Mycenae, his account of the tombs previews the finds of Schliemann. On the road that winds like a whiplash along the cliffs of the Isthmus of Corinth above the Saronic Gulf, after noting that a recent public works program under Hadrian, very similar to contemporary projects, has enabled two chariots to pass, he tells the story that is repeated by bus travelers staring down the sheer rock-splintered drop today: here the brigand Skiron waylaid wayfarers, throwing their bodies to a sea-tortoise that floated below with poised expectant flippers, until Theseus freed traffic by in turn tossing Skiron to the sea.

The continuous bringing of new sites into comprehensible form pervades Greece with a feeling of the imminence of discovery. The mood is heightened by intermittent but frequent finds of superb single statues.

The Venus de Milo came out of her mid-Aegean cave in 1820; the Victory of Samothrace was found on her forbidding northern island in 1863; the Charioteer was unearthed at Delphi in 1896.

The plowman, the shepherd, and the fisherman, and latterly the city workman, all happen upon illustrious finds. In Crete, it was a countryman whose first name was Minos who in 1878 found, among the vineyards growing above the Palace of Knossos, initial evidence of the location of that center of Minoan culture. The Museum at Rhodes displays a marble Venus that in 1929, like her mythological original, rose from the sea.

In the dangerous straits at Artemision, between Euboia and Attica, and in the similarly dangerous straits at the tip of the Peloponnese, nets cast for fish have frequently brought in bronzes, perhaps the spoils of pillagers shipwrecked some two thousand years ago. Among bronzes in the Archaeological Museum at Athens, the Little Jockey of the second century B.C. came from Artemision; the statue of Zeus—or is it Poseidon?—likewise broke water there, in 1928; farther down the same strait,

near Marathon, a bronze boy was found, dating from the late fourth century B.C. The youth with upraised arm and hand that just released an object was brought up in the south, off Antikythera, in 1900.

Even in Pausanias' day, fishermen were lucky about statues. Of Theagenes, a Thasian athlete who had won a grand total of fourteen hundred crowns at the various games, he tells:

> "When he departed this world, one of the men who had been at enmity with him in his life came every night . . . and whipped the bronze figure as if he were maltreating Theagenes himself. The statue checked his insolence by falling on him; but the sons of the deceased prosecuted the statue for murder. The Thasians sunk the statue in the sea, herein following the view taken by Draco, who, in the laws touch-

ing homicide which he drew up for the Athenians, enacted that even lifeless things should be banished if they fell on anybody and killed him. But in course of time, their land yielding them no fruits, the Thasians sent envoys to Delphi, and the god told them to bring back the exiles. The exiles were accordingly brought back, but their restoration brought no cessation of the dearth. So they went to the Pythian priestess a second time. . . . Then the Pythian priestess answered them:

" 'But you have forgotten your great Theagenes.' While they were at a loss to know how they should recover the statue of Theagenes, it is said that some fishermen who had gone a-fishing on the sea caught the statue in their net and brought it back to land."

Most recently, the finds of laborers employed on public works projects have been the most spectacular. It was work by the highway department that in 1861 located the Kerameikos at the Dipylon Gate where the road from the Peiraeus enters Athens. It was work on the Larissa subway station in 1948 that uncovered the life-sized relief of a spirited stallion with a panther skin for a saddle, pulling away from an Ethiopian groom who is struggling to tame him, now to be seen in the Archaeological Museum. And it was repair of a Peiraeus sewer in 1959 that brought to light a cache of bronze and marble statues including the earliest life-size Greek bronze so far discovered.

On this find, archaeologists have turned detective to good purpose. About eight o'clock on Saturday morning, July 18, 1959, two workmen, taking up the pavement at a busy street intersection near the Peiraeus port, noticed the bronze fingers of a hand sticking out of the dirt. Quickly, an archaeologist was summoned. Equally quickly, without summons, a contingent of sidewalk superintendents surrounded the hole. All day long, the process of uncovering continued. By late afternoon, a truck snailed its way through the crowd to transport two bronze statues, of a man and a woman, and a marble Herm—a post crowned with the head of Hermes—to the Peiraeus Archaeological Museum.

During the next week, digging continued; on the following Saturday a second major find included a bronze statue of Athena, eyes inlaid in semiprecious stones, head adorned with a magnificent crested helmet decorated with a serpent, two winged griffins, and two owls; a bronze Artemis with a quiver of arrows; a second Herm; a Hellenistic marble statue; and a large bronze mask like those used by tragic actors.

All the bronze statues are originals, not late Greek or Roman copies; they illustrate major periods of Greek art. The bronze *kouros* (young man) is an Apollo of the sixth century B.C.; of him Sappho might have written the wedding song of which the remaining fragment runs:

> *Bridegroom dear, to what shall I compare thee?*
> *To a slim green rod best do I compare thee.*

The three other bronzes date from the fourth century: the Athena of the Attic school of Praxiteles' time gives an impression, highly unusual among representations of Greek gods, of pity and concern; one arm is outstretched, the eyes look down with tenderness. Her protective attitude was underscored by the position in which she was found: the little Artemis, only five feet tall, lay close to the seven-foot Athena, with one arm around her skirt, for all the world like a frightened child.

The Herms are late copies of fifth century marbles, perhaps imitating a famous piece by Alcamenes, in Athens.

Two pieces of evidence indicate how this cache came to be where it was found. A layer of charcoal and ashes, interspersed with fragments of roof tiles, covered one of the first statues to be unearthed, and several of the bronze surfaces were fire-blackened; a commercial stoa of the ancient harbor, with the statues stored in it, apparently went up in flames. When?

A coin found in the ruins, bearing the joint symbols of Athens and of Mithridates King of Pontus, is of an issue known to have been minted in 87–86 B.C. This date, in turn, explains the fire.

For in 86 B.C., the Roman general Sulla attacked Athens for siding with Mithridates in an effort to throw off the yoke of Rome. Plutarch, in his *Life of Sulla*, gives details:

> "Sylla had a vehement and an implacable desire to conquer Athens, whether out of emulation, fighting as it were against the shadow of the once famous city, or out of anger, at the foul words and scurrilous jests with which the tyrant Aristion, showing himself daily, with unseemly gesticulations, upon the walls, had provoked him and Metella. . . .
>
> "In the meantime, news came to Sylla that some old men, talking in the Ceramicus, had been overheard to blame the tyrant for not securing the passages and approaches near the Heptachalcum, the one point where the enemy might easily get over. Sylla neglected not the report, but going in the night, and discovering the place to be assailable, set instantly to work. . . . There was no numbering the slain; the amount is to this day conjectured only from the space of the ground overflowed with blood. . . .
>
> "Not long after, Sylla won the Piraeus, and burnt most of it; amongst the rest, Philo's arsenal, a work very greatly admired."

The cache would appear to be loot, gathered to enhance the general's triumph on his return to Rome, but consumed at the warehouse before it could be shipped.

Thus today's traveler who goes to Greece to make his personal discoveries visits a land where discovery, by land or sea, is in the very air.

CHAPTER 3 *Athens: The End and the Beginning*

ATHENS is the place no traveler would keep from his schedule; it is also his point of departure for most of the rest of Greece.

The modern city has in recent years been in an upheaval of expansion. Renewal of the central section, from the laying of broad sidewalks in the café areas to the retouching of the late nineteenth century grandeurs of the pseudo-sphinxes at the Hotel Grande Bretagne, has gone on in the midst of the flooding tourist trade that funnels through Syntagma Square. Here is where the new arrival takes his first look around.

Syntagma means constitution; the square takes its name from the fact that the first Greek constitution was read from the balcony of the old Royal Palace, now the seat of the Greek Parliament, which forms the east side of the square.

27

In front of the building, soldiers in the traditional evzone dress—tasseled fez, white blouse with black slashed-sleeve jacket, short white pleated skirt, white tights and black pomponed shoes—guard the tomb of the Unknown Soldier. The tomb is a poignant reminder of the extra pall described by Thucydides, in his Periclean funeral oration for the dead of Marathon:

"one empty bier is decorated and carried in the procession: this is for the missing, whose bodies could not be recovered."

The Parliament grounds are an extensive public garden, with shaded walks gratefully filled during the heat of the day, when the noon break closes offices.

The present Royal Palace is east of this garden, as are a number of embassies, on Herodes Atticus Street. The Benaki Museum is on its extension to the north. The Greek Foreign Office and numerous embassies are on Queen Sophie Avenue, which flanks the Parliament building; the street leads out to the museum in the lovely former residence of the Duchess of Placentia, where connoisseurs find a superbly mounted display of Byzantine art and architecture.

Here, the development of Byzantine church architecture is made graphic by reconstructions of a fifth century basilica, a twelfth century church in the Greek Cross pattern, a post-Byzantine chapel.

Architectural details are also individually illustrated: pillars and screens carved in stone or wood show the change from the extruded ornamentation of the Corinthian columns of the Graeco-Roman period to the designs incised in smooth surfaces of Byzantine sculpture.

A wide-ranging exhibit of ikons, arranged chronologically, presents Orthodox use of religious imagery.

The collection of fabrics, altar cloths, and vestments includes an epitaphios from Thessalonika dating from the fourteenth century A.D.

Athens: The End and the Beginning

The Greek word for tomb is *taphos*; the design of the altar cloth called an epitaphios shows, enclosed within a decorated border, the body of the dead Christ in the tomb, surrounded by guardian angels. To permit veneration from Good Friday through Easter eve, an altar set up in the center of the church is covered by the epitaphios.

Byzantine churches, dating from the tenth to twelfth century and in current use, can be seen a few blocks west of Syntagma Square. Here too is the twelfth century "Little Cathedral"—its façade measures thirty-seven by thirty-two feet—for which stones and monuments from classical days provided much of the building material; the immediately adjacent modern Greek Orthodox cathedral, seat of the Metropolitan of Athens, is a contrast in size.

To the northwest of the square, along Churchill and Venizelos Streets, further hotels and tourist bureaus, ministries, banks, and the university line the way as far as Omonoia Square.

Thus is comprised the central area of Athens the magnet, the new source of life and livelihood which has continually drawn more and more Greeks away from agricultural areas of niggardly yields and from stony islands until, of a total Greek population of some 8.2 million, about 1.4 million live in the nation's capital. Many Athenians maintain local loyalties elsewhere: for example, nearly five thousand people consider themselves citizens of the island of Mykonos, though only three out of five of them actually live there; the others follow the sea or live in Athens, returning for the great feast days of the church, for vacations, or for family gatherings at funerals or weddings.

This is also the area of Athens the hub: more often than not, the traveler's itinerary will follow one radius out from the capital to the coast and then return to follow another. Tickets for all forms of transportation—buses, railroads, airlines, shipping—to places within Greece as well as outside, are obtained in the offices around Syntagma Square.

Here are the bureaus from which airport buses leave for the hour and three quarters flight to Corfu, the hour and twenty minute flight to Crete, the hour and a half flight to Rhodes, as well as for foreign destinations. Here are the offices, with knowledgeable and multilingual guides, where bookings are made for the bus tours arranged by the Greek government.

Available tours range from excursions around the city of Athens or an afternoon run to Cape Sounion on the southeast Attic coast to comprehensive visits of up to six days, with all services provided. The latter make readily accessible the main sites of ancient Greece—Delphi, Olympia, Sparta, Argos, Mycenae, Corinth—as well as notable Byzantine monuments, from nearby Daphni to Mistra in the Peloponnese or the Meteora in the north. Combinations can be suited to the traveler's time and to the intensity of his interest.

Without such services, a number of places which every visitor wants to see might appear inaccessible—the country is rugged, and while mileages are relatively short, the time required to cover them over mountainous country is long. But whether he thinks in terms of a single-minded trip to Delphi or a longer circuit that ranges from Jannina to Olympia, with present facilities no traveler need be intimidated by geography.

At the tourist agencies, private cars, with or without chauffeurs and private guides, can likewise be hired, either for out-of-the-way destinations, or for higher-priced privacy on more traveled routes.

In the Syntagma Square area, too, passages can be booked for sea transport on boats departing from the Peiraeus port that lies twenty minutes south of Athens by interurban electric railway or taxicab.

Cruise ships visit a variety of islands in leisurely sequences, with itineraries running as far as the Dalmatian coast to the northwest, or all the way to Rhodes to the east; passengers live on board and debark to sight-see while their ship lies at anchor. Since many islands—Crete, for instance—have a number of charming ports, a cruise ship offers a means of seeing them with less effort than is required for travel overland.

Excursion steamers make quick short runs from the Peiraeus to the nearby islands of the Saronic Gulf.

Regular passenger boats, with first- and third-class accommodations, filled with Greek businessmen, families, pilgrims, priests, as well as visitors, provide local means of circulation; they facilitate island-hopping at will, with housing found ashore on the visitor's own initiative.

Private shipping, like cars, can also be rented, ranging in size and price from an elaborate yacht to a simple caique with inboard motor and sail.

In all cases, however, the rapid rise of the tourist trade makes early placement of reservations, whether for rooms in Athens or on the islands, for bus tours or for places on boats, an increasing necessity in the main tourist seasons.

Once his business with the tourist bureaus and the banks is out of the way, the traveler is free to turn to the north and south of this central area, to the parts of Athens that contain marvels of antique Greece. Northeast of Omonoia Square, on 28th October Street, is the National Archaeological Museum. South of the city center are the Acropolis, the Hephaisteion, the Agora; the various monuments—theaters, Temple of Zeus, Arch of Hadrian—completed in their present form in Roman times; and the stadium, rebuilt for the first performance when the Olympic Games were revived in 1896.

THE NATIONAL ARCHAEOLOGICAL MUSEUM

AT most sites—Delphi, Olympia, Delos, Rhodes— the most precious finds are located in immediately adjacent museums. Minoan treasures of Crete are displayed at only a slight remove, in the museum at Heraklion.

But there are two exceptions. One comprises the Greek art—many of the best vases, some of the best statuary—that was taken abroad before today's strict laws on private purchase and removal of antiquities; it is now found in museums and private collections from Moscow to San Francisco.

The other exception is the concentration of superb pieces in the Archaeological Museum of Athens. Here, three sources of artifacts are represented: finds made in and near the capital; finds made elsewhere, either in places where there is no museum, or was none at the time of the discovery (in the latter case, returns are continually in process); and finds of objects too valuable to subject to the hazards of provincial protection. These last include the golden treasure of the Mycenean age.

At the threshold of the newly enlarged building across the flowered garden that fronts 28th October Street, one should perhaps pause to reflect on how to see a museum, particularly one of the greatest, where soft-colored settings and unobtrusive rooms encourage reflection and where an additional harmony of exposition results from the way the articles are arranged.

The way into a museum is not through its catalogue. Of the guide-book words that pack names into paragraphs, studded with stars and stressed with italics, it can indeed be said that words fail. Such books indicate what is there, certify what scholars declare to be the best. But those who, thumb and index finger carefully in place, mechanically follow the text from case to case and room to room deserve to emerge tired—and they do emerge tired—alike of foot and eye. Mostly they are tiresome types, competitively documenting themselves for encounters with others of their kind, and merit no sympathy. In advance, one can hear their gritty voices: "Well, of course I saw that, but did you see . . .?" Check lists do not add to the store of memories that need no subsequent refreshing.

But there are other words. Whoever is really to see, rather than just to look at the artifacts of the Archaeological Museum must come with an eye that has been strengthened by an inner lens, able, with magnified understanding, to observe minute detail, penetrating the carvings, the inlays, the metal work; to welcome, in the designs on the vases, the evidence of the otherwise lost Greek art of painting; to comprehend the conventions and the struggles with technique and media of the early sculptors and to sense the symmetries of later ones.

The words that are of aid in preparation for this kind of seeing are words such as Homer's account of the shield of Achilles at the end of the eighteenth book of the *Iliad,* or Hesiod's poem on the "Shield of Herakles." Both describe work by Hephaistos, armorer of the gods; they tell how, from the center to the rim which represented the ocean-river around the world, his shields were solidly covered with fine-wrought figures in bronze, tin, silver and gold. Gods, heroes, humans all were there: the works and days of ordinary life, fights with animals, fights with men, ploughing and harvesting, death and dances. Singly or in combination, these are the very scenes that are portrayed on and by the cups, vases, weapons, friezes, statues, steles that have survived the centuries and are now assembled in Athens. To them, Homer's description of the shield of Achilles is a guide of a different order:

> "He began by making a large and powerful shield, adorned all over, finished with a bright triple rim of gleaming metal, and fitted with a silver baldric. The shield consisted of five layers, and he decorated the face of it with a number of designs, executed with consummate skill and representing, first of all, Earth, Sky and Sea, and the indefatigable Sun, the Moon at the full, and all the Constellations with which the heavens are crowned, the Pleiads, the Hyads, the great Orion, and the Bear, nicknamed the Wain, the only constellation which never bathes in Ocean Stream, but always wheels round in the same place and looks across at Orion the Hunter with a wary eye.

"Next he showed two beautiful cities full of people. In one of them weddings and banquets were afoot. They were bringing the brides through the streets from their homes, to the loud music of the wedding hymn and the light of blazing torches. Youths accompanied by flute and lyre were whirling in the dance, and the women had come to the doors of their houses to enjoy the show. But the men had flocked to the meeting-place, where a case had come up between two litigants, about the payment of compensation for a man who had been killed. The defendant claimed the right to pay in full and was announcing his intention to the people; but the other contested his claim and refused all compensation. Both parties insisted that the issue should be settled by a referee; and both were cheered by their supporters in the crowd, whom the heralds were attempting to silence. The Elders sat on the sacred bench, a semicircle of polished stone; and each, as he received the speaker's rod from the clear-voiced heralds, came forward in his turn to give his judgment staff in hand. Two talents of gold were displayed in the centre: they were the fee for the Elder whose exposition of the law should prove the best.

"The other city was beleaguered by two armies, which were shown in their glittering equipment. The besiegers were unable to agree whether to sack the place outright—it was a lovely town—or to divide all the moveable property it contained between themselves and the inhabitants. But these had not yet capitulated: they were secretly preparing for an ambush. Leaving the walls defended by their wives and little children, together with the older men, they sallied forth under the leadership of Ares and Pallas Athene, who were both shown in gold. Fully armed and dressed in golden clothes, they were big and beautiful as gods should be, and stood out above their troops, who were of smaller build. When they had found a likely place for an ambush, in a river-bed where all the cattle came to drink, they sat down there in their shining bronze, after posting two scouts in the distance to watch for the coming of the sheep and the cattle with their crooked horns. These soon appeared, in charge of two herdsmen, who were playing on their pipes,

34

suspecting no evil. The ambushed men caught sight of them, dashed out and promptly headed off the herds of oxen and the fine flocks of white sheep, killing the shepherds. But when the besiegers, who were sitting in debate, heard the commotion raised by this affair among the herds, they mounted at once behind their high-stepping horses and made for the scene of action, which they quickly reached. A pitched battle ensued on the banks of the river, and volleys of bronze spears were exchanged. Strife and Panic were shown at their work, and there was the dreadful Spirit of Death laying her hands on a freshly wounded man who was still alive and another not yet wounded, and dragging a corpse by its foot through the crowd. The cloak on her shoulders was red with human blood, and the soldiers met and fought and dragged away each other's dead like real men.

"Next he depicted a large field of soft, rich fallow, which was being ploughed for the third time. A number of ploughmen were driving their teams across it to and fro. When they reached the ridge at the end of the field and had to wheel, a man would come up and hand them a cup of mellow wine. Then they turned back down the furrows and toiled along through the deep fallow soil to reach the other end. The field, though it was made of gold, grew black behind them, as a field does when it is being ploughed. The artist had achieved a miracle.

"He also showed a king's estate, where hired reapers were at work with sharp sickles in their hands. Armfuls of corn fell down in rows along the furrow, while others were tied up with straw by the sheaf-binders. Three of these were standing by, and the boys who were gleaning behind them came running up to them with bundles in their arms and kept them constantly supplied. And there among them was the King himself, staff in hand, standing by the swathe in quiet satisfaction. Under an oak in the background his attendants were preparing a feast. They were cooking a great ox that they had slaughtered, and the women were sprinkling the meat for the labourers' supper with handfuls of white barley.

"The next scene was a vineyard laden with grapes. It was beautifully

35

wrought in gold, but the bunches themselves were black and the supporting poles showed up throughout in silver. All round it he ran a
ditch of blue enamel and outside that a fence of tin. The vineyard was
approached by a single pathway for the pickers' use at vintage time; and
the delicious fruit was being carried off in baskets by merry lads and
girls, with whom there was a boy singing the lovely song of Linus in a
treble voice to the sweet music of his tuneful lyre. They all kept time
with him and followed the music and the words with dancing feet.

"He also showed a herd of straight-horned cattle, making the cows of
gold and tin. They were mooing as they hurried from the byre to feed
where the rushes swayed beside a murmuring stream. Four golden
herdsmen accompanied the cattle, and there were nine dogs trotting
along with them. But at the head of the herd a pair of savage lions had
seized a bellowing bull, who roared aloud as they dragged him off. The
young men and dogs ran up to the rescue. But the lions had rent the
bull's hide and were lapping up his dark blood and entrails. It was in
vain that the shepherds incited and egged on their fast dogs, who had
no intention of biting the lions. They were careful to avoid them,
though they stood and barked as close as they dared.

"To this picture the illustrious lame god added a big grazing ground
for white-fleeced sheep, in a beautiful valley, complete with its farm
buildings, pens and well-roofed huts.

"Next the god depicted a dancing-floor like the one that Daedalus
designed in the spacious town of Cnossus for Ariadne of the lovely
locks. Youths and marriageable maidens were dancing on it with their
hands on one another's wrists, the girls in fine linen with lovely garlands on their heads, and the men in closely woven tunics showing the
faint gleam of oil, and with daggers of gold hanging from their silver
belts. Here they ran lightly round, circling as smoothly on their accomplished feet as the wheel of a potter when he sits and works it with his
hands to see if it will spin; and there they ran in lines to meet each
other. A large crowd stood round enjoying the delightful dance, with
a minstrel among them singing divinely to the lyre, while a couple of

acrobats, keeping time with his music, threw cart-wheels in and out among the people.

"Finally, round the very rim of the wonderful shield he put the mighty Stream of Ocean.

"When the shield was finished, in all its size and strength, he made Achilles a cuirass brighter than blazing fire. Then he made a massive helmet to fit on his temples. It was beautifully chased, and he put a golden crest on the top. He also made him greaves of pliant tin.

"When the renowned lame god had finished every piece, he gathered them up and laid them before Achilles' Mother. She took the glittering armour from Hephaestus and swooped down with it like a falcon from snow-clad Olympus."

After having listened to Homer, one can turn to the Museum better prepared to see, in the works of other artificers, the same desire to transmit, with maximum intensity and liveliness, the range of human experience, its wars and its peace, its solemnities and its convivialities, from the earliest age of prehistory through the classical period and on into Hellenistic times.

At the Museum's opening door, no one, even the least observant, could fail to feel the impact of the *coup de théâtre* administered by the gold masks that once covered the faces of dead Mycenean kings.

Here is the accoutrement of pre-Homeric and Homeric heroes. Here are the Peloponnesian finds of Heinrich Schliemann, whose uncanny nose for gold, after it had led him like a truffle dog's to dig for Priam's palace at Troy, took him off on a new scent to Argos, there to locate the citadel of the Atreides, stronghold of the leader of Priam's conquerors.

Here too are the results of later Mycenean digging by the Greek Archaeological Society and the English School, including treasures that came to light in the 1950's in the tombs that Schliemann missed.

Schliemann impetuously identified the masked personages of the tombs as Agamemnon and other members of that royal household whose lives provided both a conquering epic for the Homeric bards and a cycle of fated horrors for the Greek tragedians. And while subsequent scholarship indicates that the masks belonged not to the Atreides but to a dynasty ruling perhaps four hundred years earlier, the names remain popular.

Likewise buried with the warrior kings and their consorts: helmets of cunningly joined boars' teeth, elaborately tooled necklaces and strings of beads, carefully wrought brooch-pins to hold royal robes, deeply-carved signet rings and sealstones, finely decorated gold bowls. Interspersed among these meticulously designed items, however, are numerous little crudely painted clay images, figurines thought perhaps to be domestic tutelaries. They come in two models, and are called *phi-psi*, because the pose of one, with arms and hands looped in supplication, looks like the Greek letter Φ, and the other, with arms stretched up and out at its sides, resembles the letter Ψ. Since there are so many of them, and since the work on them is crude in comparison with that of the other artifacts, they impiously call to mind the pottery dogs, deer, and ibises of American roadside stands.

Set off by themselves in glass so that one can see both sides at eye level are unforgettably fine handles of short swords or daggers, of bronze inlaid with gold, silver, electrum and niello. The scenes decorating them are hunts: armed men attack a charging lion; a lion hunts deer; leopards stalk quail; a cheetah chases wild duck in a marsh, crashing through papyrus plants. The action is so spirited that one awaits a successor to the moment he is witnessing; it is easy to understand why Homer and Hesiod included sound and sequence in describing the god-made shields.

A little further along in the display, the *Iliad* is again called on for the name of a magnificent beaker known as "Nestor's cup." Archaeologists have located Nestor's sixty-room palace at Pylos in the southwestern Peloponnese; their finds range from records in Linear B script

to the room which may be one of the few identifiable settings described in the *Odyssey*, the throne room where Telemachus, son of Odysseus, was counselled by Nestor in the course of his search for his father; likewise uncovered was a tub that fits the description of the bath given the traveller by the great king's daughter. But the goblet in Athens, fashioned from a single sheet of gold, with two handles doubly attached to the bowl of the cup and to its base and surmounted by gold birds facing inward at the rim, derives its name only from its resemblance, in miniature, to the larger four-handled vessel which Homer affirms the old warrior brought with him to the siege of Troy. At his tent there, Hecamede served Nestor and Machaon:

> "She began by moving up to them a handsome polished table with enamelled legs. On this she put a bronze dish with an onion to flavour the drink, some yellow honey, and sacred barley-meal; and beside these a magnificent beaker adorned with golden studs, which the old man had brought from home. It had four handles. Each was supported by two legs; and on top of each, facing one another, a pair of golden doves were feeding. Anyone else would have found it difficult to shift the beaker from the table when it was full, but Nestor, old as he was, could lift it without trouble."

Another outstanding Mycenean treasure is the pair of gold cups found at Vaphio, below Sparta. The relief on one shows violent action: a hunt of wild bulls has resulted in a capture; one animal, netted and thrown on his back, is struggling to free himself, while another escapes after hurling a hunter to the ground. The companion cup exemplifies bucolic calm: two tamed bulls and a cow move peacefully while a man

holds a rope that is tied around the right hind hoof of one of the placid bulls.

Nearby are a magnificent bull's head in the form of a *rhyton*, or libation vase; a gold cup from Mideia, adorned with seascapes and dolphins; a rock crystal vase in the form of a duck—the tail forms the spout and the neck and backward-turned head the handle.

Among signet rings and sealstones one ring from Tiryns displays four lion-shaped winged monsters carrying a pitcher to a seated deity; on another, wasp-waisted goddesses are worshipped under fruited trees.

An inconspicuous but exciting item among these small objects is the head and shoulders of a statuette of a little monkey from the Acropolis of Mycenae, found in 1896. On his diminutive shoulder is a tiny yellow cartouche, which dates him; he was made in the time of Pharaoh Amenophis II, about 1450 B.C. As soon as the cartouche was recognized, the little statue took on the proportions of a historic bench mark. Its presence not only confirmed the fact of contact between the contemporary civilizations of the years 1900–1400 B.C. in Egypt and mainland Greece; by means of it, the dynasty that built Mycenae could be superimposed upon the scale of time.

All of this splendor from prehistory is in the first room of the Museum. Beyond, rooms of statuary, marble and bronze; reliefs and steles; vase collections; figurines, represent the art of the centuries following the in-migration to the area of the various peoples who together comprised the historic Greeks.

There are many ways to view these exhibits. The least sophisticated is to consider a single statue, a single vase, by itself, unrelated to time or circumstance, as an isolated embodiment of beauty, with the viewing a direct experience unrelated to all others: it was a coin of the Sicilian city of Gela that, a generation ago, initiated my interest in Greece.

For a time, such a view can be enough. But any object, no matter how far it surpasses its contemporaries, was yet the product of time and circumstance, and eventually its placement in the stream of development can hardly fail to induce the curiosity of the viewer: known or unknown, where did this potter, this painter, this sculptor, this die-cutter belong? However broadly, either en route or before or after his trip, the traveller may wish to extend his Greek horizons—and he should not forget that to an archaeologist the word horizon connotes time as well as space—he would do well to provide himself with at least pre-liminary appreciation of the sequence of the various phases of Greek art.

To be able to place a statue in the course of development from the archaic period of noble but stylized and rigid form, through the era of greater freedom in which the artist was still struggling both with tech-nique and medium and with the concept which he wished to convey, to the time when the struggle was over and facility was soon to terminate in fanciness is to know much more about what one sees than if one sees each as a thing in itself.

To be able to identify a vase in the sequence from the use of natural-colored clay ornamented with horizontal bands of stylized geometric designs, to the use of red clay with increasingly natural figures painted in black upon it, to the reverse process by which black-painted back-grounds surrounded red figures, whose features and dress were indicated in black, is to begin an understanding which can be deepened until the viewer can distinguish sources of pottery other than Athens—the islands, Corinth, Boieotia, for example—that were gradually extinguished in the Athenian monopoly; until he can recognize the manner of the more than a hundred individual potters and painters who signed their works; until he can give an educated guess as to the earliness or lateness of a given vase within these major periods.

Once a viewer begins to place the art he sees in the stream of time, he also inevitably becomes interested in cross-sections: when a given frieze was carved, what other friezes were in the making? What temples, theaters, treasuries were recently new or currently a-building? What were the vase painters of the time selecting as favorite subjects? At the theater, who were the playwrights of the hour? Which philosophers had followings in the agora? (At the back of this book, a rudimentary table provides a start for such comparisons.)

A specialized form of observation, which can be followed both in cross-section and up and down the stream of time, is to take a single myth, a tale of a god, a story of a hero, and discover how it was treated by vase painters, coin designers, sculptors, poets and playwrights. One archaeologist has followed through the whole course of Greek art still-existing representations of Amazons. These were the often-depicted warrior women who appear in mythology in such combats as those between Herakles and Hippolyta, Achilles and Penthesilea, and in an attempted invasion of Athens after Theseus carried off their queen. From statuettes and tiny figures carved on gems, to paintings on all shapes and varieties of vases, to sculptured reliefs, friezes, metopes from temples, to life-sized statues, they are to be found in museums across the world, from Auckland to Würzberg. One's own pursuit of a chosen theme can be more limited: confined to the Archaeological Museum itself, or to the City of Athens, or to all sites visited in Greece. On the other hand, an interest so initiated is a companion on further travels, for the dispersal of Greek pottery was so wide in the days before export control that almost any great city offers new vase paintings or sculpture for further comparison.

Many of the Archaeological Museum's most striking bronzes were mentioned in an earlier chapter; others include the battered head of an old pugilist from the third century, when sculpture had turned from stylized or idealized types to individual portraiture.

Because of the greater vulnerability to destruction of marble statues, very few of these have survived from classical times: most masterpieces are known today only through verbal descriptions by such travellers as Pausanias; occasional representations in Roman frescoes such as those at Herculanaeum and Pompeii; and debased copies carved in Hellenistic or Roman times—the Museum's small and tawdry Roman version of Pheidias' huge lost statue of Athena of the Parthenon is a deplorable example. Among originals is the statue of the warrior found in the acropolis of Sparta and hence known by the name of the city's hero, Leonidas; the head of Tegea, which was once stolen from the Museum and later located in a peasant's barn, carefully preserved as the basis of a dowry for his daughter; the colossal fifth-century Apollo Patroös, discovered in the Athenian Agora.

Reliefs are much more numerous: one from Sounion shows a youth crowning himself at the games; another, from Phokis, models a child and a goose; a third, from Brauron in eastern Attica, depicts the legend of Leda and the Swan. There is a relief of Dionysos, holding his wine cup and wand, one of the healer Asklepios from Epidauros, one of a Corinthian chorus leader and two courtesans. The sides of two marble bases found in the Themistoclean wall in Athens and dating from around 500 B.C. display an animated hockey-match, chariot-racing, athletes wrestling, a dog-and-cat fight. Probably the most beautiful of the reliefs is that from Eleusis showing Demeter, whom the king of Eleusis comfortingly received in the course of her search for her daughter after Persephone was abducted by Hades to the darkness of the lower world. In appreciation, the goddess bestows a grain, symbolizing the gift of agriculture, on the king's son, the young Triptolemus.

Among the funeral steles, typical patterns are an upright slab, topped by an acanthus, with a relief of the dead person on the side of the stone, or a temple form, topped by an architrave, a pillar on each side, a family scene carved between. Many steles depict the persons who have died in some act which gave them pleasure while living. One from the fourth century shows a nude youth, dejectedly leaning on a pilaster, a

club in his left hand, a long-nosed hunting dog by his side; opposite him are a sorrowing parent and a grieving servant. On two of the most beautiful steles, Hegiso, daughter of Proxenos and wife of Koroibos, seated, selects jewels from a casket held by a standing maidservant; a man feeds a grasshopper to his dog.

Some of the corridors leading to these rooms are invigoratingly punctuated by arrogant heads of insolent bronze griffins.

Perhaps the first enjoyment among the vase collections is enjoyment of pure form, appreciation of the potter's art that underlay the painter's.

Ornamented though all but the crudest pottery is, it was not designed to be ornamental: the vases which today are prized and protected as museum pieces were made for use, though some were intended, like Western fine china, for special occasions such as might be suitable for a Lowestoft soup tureen, a Dresden punch bowl, or a Sèvres epergne.

It does not take long to recognize the main shapes: for storage of supplies, from cereal to wine, the *amphora* is a large—sometimes even a colossal—jar with handles; the *stamnos* is for the same purpose, but shorter and squatter. The *krater,* shaped rather like an inverted bell, and called a column krater when it has a base that is a standard, is the mixing bowl for water and wine; the *oinochoe,* a jug-like pitcher. The *hydria* is three-handled, a tall and graceful pitcher; it could pour out into a *kotyle,* or two-handled beaker; a *rhyton* or drinking horn, usually in the form of an animal's head; a *kylix,* a shallow plate-like goblet on a stand whose shape offers a beautifully uninterrupted surface to the painter; or a *kantharos,* a wine cup with high handles curving in the loveliest of lines. A *phiale* is a shallow bowl for libations.

Athletes kept the oil with which they rubbed themselves in a variety of narrow-necked containers: the tall, slender one-handled pitcher called a *lekythos*—a form which was likewise often used for funeral vases for young men; or smaller, more compact containers, the *alabastron,* the *aryballos,* the *askos.* The lady's *pyxis* was a round toilet box for unguents—there is a vase by the Achilles painter which shows a young girl carrying one.

Observation of the decoration which the painters of successive periods applied to these shapes leads off in two directions—to the real and to the unreal.

There is delight in the unreal creatures which file across the decorative bands of vases from many periods, especially the earlier centuries when, possibly because the artists were influenced by Oriental fabrics, every bit of space was filled with form. Among them are chimeras, sphinxes (Greek sphinxes, unlike their Egyptian counterparts, do not lie down, they sit up attentively), winged horses, gorgons, sirens, centaurs, satyrs, the goat-god Pan; then there are the vases ornamented with two pairs of huge disembodied eyes.

On the anthropomorphic borderline of unreality are the Olympians, Zeus, Athena, Apollo, the entire Greek theogony, mostly engaged in doings all too familiar to humanity, from the *pelike* showing Hades with a horn of plenty and Demeter with a plow to the *pyxis* on which Poseidon pursues the Danaïd Amymone.

Still closer to reality are the superhuman heroes such as Herakles and Theseus, with their multitudinous labors and exploits in excess of the powers of ordinary men. One spirited fragment of a bowl from Pharsala in Thessaly, made in the first quarter of the sixth century, shows a grandstandful of gesticulating heroes watching the chariot race at the funeral games of Patroclus. Another, made a generation later by one of the potter-painters who signed his work, displays Achilles preparing his celebrated horses for battle. A favorite heroic subject is the hunt of the Calydonian boar: an amphora shows the flower of Greece responding to the call for help of the king of Calydon, whose land was being ravaged by a terrible creature sent by Artemis because she had been forgotten in the sacrifice of the first fruits at harvest time. Among red-figured vases, a hydria shows how Orithyea, daughter of King Erech-

47

theus of Athens, was swept away by Boreas, the North Wind, after her father had refused him her hand. The god's huge wings are supplemented by winged boots; hair and beard windblown, he seizes the maiden as she is running towards an altar, her left hand out and her head turned back toward her pursuer.

From the real world come the familiar animals, the dolphins, the octapods, the deer, the lions, the boars, the dogs, and above all the horses. Xenophon, drawing on a still earlier source of which no manuscript remains, wrote, in the earliest existing treatise on dressage riding: "It is upon horses of this kind that gods and heroes are painted riding, and men who are able to manage them skilfully are regarded as deserving of admiration. So extremely beautiful, and admirable, and noble a sight is a horse that bears himself superbly, that he fixes the gaze of all who see him, . . ." The Homeric and heroic legends recount the genealogy and the qualities of famous named mares—often bred by the North Wind and like the wind in fleetness—and their foals, ridden, or driven in twos or fours to the two-wheeled chariot, and the Museum has vase painting, friezes and statues of their descendants down the centuries.

The human realities are portrayed in spirited versions of the works and days of Greek life: tradesmen at their trades—the potter, the painter, the shoemaker, the foundryman, the oil dealer, the baker; customers making purchases from various merchants; girls drawing water at the fountain; men mixing and cooling wine, enjoying a drinking party, suffering a hangover; athletes at games; women engaged in household tasks, spinning, cooking, gathering apples.

At least, they gather the apples that are within reach. For some, they must wait for windfall—one of the luckiest windfalls in Greek poetry is the fragment from Sappho that Rossetti translated:

> *Like the sweet apple which reddens upon the topmost bough,*
> *A-top the topmost twig,—which the pluckers forgot somehow,—*
> *Forgot it not, nay, but got it not, for none could get it till now.*

The liveliness of all of the vases is a ceaseless wonder; perhaps the words of Keats' *Ode to a Grecian Urn* best capture the arrested motion of the great vase-painters' art:

> *Fair youth, beneath the trees, thou canst not leave*
> *Thy song, nor ever can those trees be bare;*
>   *Bold lover, never, never canst thou kiss,*
> *Though winning near the goal—yet, do not grieve;*
> *She cannot fade, though thou hast not thy bliss,*
> *For ever wilt thou love, and she be fair!*

But among the human realities is also the reality of death, the recurrent poignant memorials to those who, more often than not, died young. The funeral vases include a ninth century amphora whose stylized horizontal bands of geometric decoration are interrupted for the

49

presentation of a funeral procession in which black figures with arms above their heads precede and follow a body borne on a bier. On a jar from an Athenian grave of the seventh century Herakles kills the centaur Nessos: under guise of carrying Herakles' wife across a river dry-shod, the creature had attempted to violate her; below the rectangle depicting this scene, gorgons and dolphins frolic over the sea; the edge of the lip and the handles of the jar are decorated with birds.

The collective tomb of the Athenians who died at Marathon in 490 B.C. yielded a number of black-figured vases. On one of these, Herakles supports the skies while Atlas brings him the apples of the Hesperides; on another, satyrs engage in a wild dance.

Perhaps the most beautiful of the funeral vases are the white-ground lekythoi made in the latter part of the fifth century. These are painted in romantic, almost Byronic style; the graceful figures, outlined by thin black lines, have auburn hair. A number show young men seated at their tombs. On one with several figures, a warrior is seated with his wife standing at his left and a youth at his right; on another, a soldier, with crested helmet and round shield emblazoned with a huge eye drawn in profile, is taking leave of a seated woman.

Latest in time among the vases is a group showing languorous ladies, in elaborately draped chitons and himations and with complicated hair-dos, seated or standing holding mirrors in self-admiration, and attended by Eros, the little winged love. Actual bronze mirrors and mirror stands such as those depicted are also part of the collection, together with items from Greek festal boards.

What the mirrors reflected in earlier periods can be gathered from the Tanagra figurines: the thoughtful woman, seated; the two friends; the woman—could it have been Lysistrata—who has a slight air of presiding officer.

During the classical period, with the exception of certain great courtesans like Aspasia, the companion of Pericles, or Lais of Corinth,

Greek women were relegated to a position of sheltered inconspicuousness. Customs differed from city-state to city-state; Athens was stricter than most. In the Periclean funeral oration, the Athenian widows of Marathon are advised:

"If I must also speak a word to those who are now in widowhood on the powers and duties of women, I will cast all my advice into one brief sentence. Great will be your glory if you do not lower the nature that is within you—hers greatest of all whose praise or blame is least bruited on the lips of men."

Men prevalently had favorites of their own sex; in Roman times, when Hadrian outlived the young Antinoös memorial statues to him were erected around the empire—one is in the museum at Delphi.

It was a woman writing of a woman when Sappho said:

> Some say a host of horsemen, others of infantry, and
>   others of ships, it is the most beautiful thing in
>   the dark earth: but I say, it is what you love.
> Full easy it is to make this understood of one and
>   all: for she that far surpasseth all mortals in
>   beauty, Helen, her most noble husband
> Deserted, and went sailing to Troy, with never a
>   thought for her daughter and dear parents. The
>   ... led her from the path ...
>   ... now has put me in mind of Anactoria far away;
> Her lovely way of walking, and the bright radiance
>   of her changing face, would I rather see than your
>   Lydian chariots and infantry full armed.

So in the real world, the position of women contrasts sharply with the prominence and initiative of the Greek goddesses, and the importance of women in the heroic legends, though Aristophanes, in his *Lysistrata* and *Thesmophoriazusai*, indicates clearly that the battle of the sexes was not confined to the Olympians.

THE AGORA

NOT only in the Western world but in today's new areas of self-governing consciousness, the architecture of most government buildings derives from Greece. The design of its columns may range from plain to fancy, drawing on any of the three basic orders, Doric, Ionic, or Corinthian; but it traces back to forms newly developed on this Mediterranean peninsula when history was young.

The institutions housed inside these buildings are no less derived from the new forms of government which took shape in the compact, controlled environment of the Greek city-state. Aristotle's collection of constitutions of Greek city-states includes 158 basic documents, but the history of Athens at its great moment can be taken as a prototype.

The first beginnings took place when the powers of the kingships of the heroic period gradually devolved upon archons who acted in the name of the king in performing military, civil, and religious offices. Exercise of these functions by members of aristocratic families led to usurpations. The Draconian laws established in 621 B.C. codified procedure for an aristocratic society, but in such severe form as to incite unrest among the oppressed lower classes.

At the beginning of the sixth century, Solon modified and softened these laws, established a Council of Four Hundred, and instituted popular courts. He divided the inhabitants of Attica into four classes, of which the rulers formed the highest, the others being the men of the hills, the plain, and the shore.

A generation later, the tyrant Peisistratos seized power, backed by the

53

men of the hills who wanted land reform, against the men of the plain and of the shore. Twice in control after 560, and twice driven out by coalitions, in 541 Peisistratos established himself firmly and ruled well until his death in 527.

While he saw to it that major posts were consistently held by members of his family, the forms of Solon's constitution and the rule of law as between man and man were retained, and since his opposition came from aristocratic sources, he found advantage in the enhancement of less well-placed groups.

His military policy was one of good relations with all surrounding city-states, lest they be used as staging areas by his enemies. The economic base of Athens in his time was broadened by his control of the silver mines at Pangaion and Laurion during the years when the invention of coinage was transforming Mediterranean trade: the archaic owl design adopted for the first Athenian coinage was retained because it became a recognized symbol from Spain and Tunis to the Tigris and the Indus. In his *Birds*, Aristophanes prophesies that

> *First, then, in your empty coffers you shall see*
> *the sterling Owl,*
> *From the mines of Laurium, familiar as a common*
> *fowl,*
> *Roosting among his bags and pouches, each at ease*
> *upon his nest:*
> *Undisturb'd, rearing and hatching little broods*
> *of interest.*

Athens: The End and the Beginning

Peisistratos initiated a large public works program: on the Acropolis he built the old temple of Athena, the Hekatompedon, whose architectural sculpture can be seen in the Museum there today. He instituted both the quadrennial Panathenaic festival and the annual Dionysiac rites from whose representations drama developed. He is thought to have been the patron who caused the Homeric epics, composed and transmitted mouth to mouth by bards over the preceding several centuries, to be set down in written form.

The sons of Peisistratos proved far less able than their father; after their deposition, there were confused years in Athens until Kleisthenes took power toward the end of the sixth century and set up a democratic state. He divided the people of Attica into ten *demes* or tribes—a number later increased to twelve. First by lot and later by ballot, each deme chose fifty representatives to form a five-hundred-man Council or *Boule*. These groups served in rotation as the city's executive, with some of their members always on duty to assure the people of an unsleeping authority; they likewise provided chairmen for the committees of the Council. The entire free native adult male populace formed the Athenian Assembly.

Kleisthenes further inaugurated a board of ten generals—the *strategoi*—to secure the city's defense.

Shortly after the adoption of this new form of government, foreign invasion subjected it to a harsh test of survival.

During the sixth century, Croesus, King of Lydia, subjugated the Greek city-states of Asia Minor. Cyrus, King of Persia, then dethroned Croesus and enlarged his empire around the eastern Mediterranean to include not only Asia Minor but Egypt. The next Persian thrust, under Cyrus' son Darius, was an attempt to enter Europe. In 499 B.C., when Darius was thus occupied, the Asia Minor cities attempted a revolt. Athens and Eretria sent them aid, but the effort failed. Thereafter, according to legend, Darius had a servant remind him before each meal to "remember the Athenians." A first expedition to punish them failed en route, but a second one successfully landed troops at Marathon, northeast of Athens, in 490 B.C. There the Greek forces, against great odds, defeated them.

In 480, Darius' son Xerxes tried again. At Thermopylae, three hundred heroic Spartans died in a holding operation, after which the Persian forces went on to Athens, but in the ensuing sea battle at Salamis the Athenian fleet justified the new naval policy of whose soundness Themistocles had persuaded his fellow citizens in the nick of time. A land action under Spartan leadership next year at Plataea definitely ended the Persian threat.

Not too long thereafter the Athenians exiled Themistocles for arrogance, and Kleisthenes' grandnephew, Pericles, became the dominant figure on the Athenian political scene. He held office only as one of the board of *strategoi*, but from the 460's until his death of plague in 429, he set the city's main directions.

This was the great age: architecture, painting, theater, political science, philosophy, mathematics flowered in the new freedom.

The historian Thucydides, writing at the end of the century when the political pre-eminence of Athens was over, cast in the form of a funeral oration by Pericles a eulogy of the spirit of the Athenian government:

" . . . Of the battles which we and our fathers fought, whether in the winning of our power abroad or in bravely withstanding the warfare of barbarian or Greek at home, I do not wish to say more: they are too familiar to you all. I wish rather to set forth the spirit in which we faced them, and the constitution and manners with which we rose to greatness, and to pass from them to the dead; for I think it not unfitting that these things should be called to mind at today's solemnity, and expedient too that the whole gathering of citizens and strangers should listen to them.

Athens: The End and the Beginning

"For our government is not copied from those of our neighbours: we are an example to them rather than they to us. Our constitution is named a democracy, because it is in the hands not of the few but of the many. But our laws secure equal justice for all in their private disputes, and our public opinion welcomes and honours talent in every branch of achievement, not for any sectional reason but on grounds of excellence alone. And as we give free play to all in our public life, so we carry the same spirit into our daily relations with one another. We have no black looks or angry words for our neighbour if he enjoys himself in his own way, and we abstain from the little acts of churlishness which, though they leave no mark, yet cause annoyance to whoso notes them. Open and friendly in our private intercourse, in our public acts we keep strictly within the control of law. We acknowledge the restraint of reverence; we are obedient to whomsoever is set in authority, and to the laws, more especially to those which offer protection to the oppressed and those unwritten ordinances whose transgression brings admitted shame.

"Yet ours is no work-a-day city only. No other provides so many recreations for the spirit—contests and sacrifices all the year round, and beauty in our public buildings to cheer the heart and delight the eye day by day. Moreover, the city is so large and powerful that all the wealth of all the world flows in to her, so that our own Attic products seem no more homelike to us than the fruits of the labours of other nations.

"Our military training too is different from our opponents'. The gates of our city are flung open to the world. We practice no periodical deportations, nor do we prevent our visitors from observing or discovering what an enemy might usefully apply to his own purposes. For our trust is not in the devices of material equipment, but in our own good spirits for battle.

"So too with education. They [the Spartans] toil from early boyhood in a laborious pursuit after courage, while we, free to live and wander as we please, march out none the less to face the self-same dangers. . . .

57

"We are lovers of beauty without extravagance, and lovers of wisdom without unmanliness. Wealth to us is not mere material for vainglory but an opportunity for achievement; and poverty we think it no disgrace to acknowledge but a real degradation to make no effort to overcome. Our citizens attend both to public and private duties, and do not allow absorption in their own various affairs to interfere with their knowledge of the city's. We differ from other states in regarding the man who holds aloof from public life not as 'quiet' but as useless: we decide or debate, carefully and in person, all matters of policy, holding, not that words and deeds go ill together, but that acts are foredoomed to failure when undertaken undiscussed. . . .

"In a word, I claim that our city as a whole is an education to Greece, and that her members yield to none, man by man, for independence of spirit, many-sidedness of attainment, and complete self-reliance in limbs and brain. . . .

"Such then is the city for whom, lest they should lose her, the men whom we celebrate died a soldier's death: and it is but natural that all of us, who survive them, should wish to spend ourselves in her service. That, indeed, is why I have spent many words upon the city. I wished to show that we have more at stake than men who have no such inheritance, and to support my praise of the dead by making clear to you what they have done. . . ."

But the foreign policy of Athens did not permit the maintenance of this city. Related events combined to speed the end of political independence. Following the defeat of the Persians, the Aegean islands had been organized under Athenian leadership into a confederation to resist future attack, with the island of Delos serving as the confederation's center. Members contributed money or ships. In 454 Pericles, to the resentment of the other member states, removed to Athens from Delos the treasure of the Delian Confederation, and used some of it to build the Parthenon. In 431, the commercial rivalry between Athens and Corinth, with Corinth supported by Sparta, culminated in the First

Athens: The End and the Beginning

Peloponnesian War. Immediately after the conclusion of an uneasy peace, in 415 Athens undertook an attack upon Syracuse in Sicily, then the second-ranking Greek city. The expedition ended in disastrous defeat; its leader, Alcibiades, turned traitor and went over to Sparta; the war began again. In 405, the Athenian grain fleet, on its way back from the Black Sea, was demolished off Thrace in the battle of Aegospotamoi. Athens surrendered to Sparta the next year.

The Spartan hegemony lasted until 371, when the Theban general Epaminondas invented the wedge to replace the phalanx in offensive tactics, and defeated the Spartans at Leuctra. But Theban pre-eminence was short-lived. In an effort to extend this victory Epaminondas was killed while winning the battle of Mantinea nine years later, and the league which Thebes had headed fell apart.

The next coherent rule in Greece was established by a foreigner, Philip of Macedon. Demosthenes, in his Philippic orations, tried to rouse the Athenian Assembly to the coming danger, but in 338, near Thebes, the battle of Chaironeia gave Philip control of Greece.

Many of the greatnesses of Athens outlasted the period of its political independence. When Pericles came to power, Socrates was one of the youths of Athens; until his death at the age of seventy, he taught the best of his philosophical successors. In the end, he was accused of corrupting the young—arguing them away from democratic principles—and of irreligion; the account of his trial, defense, and condemnation transmitted by his younger associate, Plato, witnesses both the method of teaching by dialogue which gave the Agora its intellectual brilliance during the great period, and the philosophy of man and the state developed by this master-and-pupil interchange.

In the fourth century, development in all the arts went on: Greece and Athens were adorned by Praxiteles, Scopas, and Lysippus in art, Menander in comedy, Theodotus and Polyclitus the Younger in architecture, and a whole generation of philosophers and historians.

For while Socrates' execution in 399 forced his philosophical asso-

ATHENS

THE AGORA AND ITS ENVIRONS

IN THE SECOND CENTURY A.D.

ciates into temporary retirement, in 387 Plato, who was born the year
that Pericles died, founded the Academy, and presided over it until his
own death about 348. Plato's reflections on the nature of good government and the good life, in his *Republic* and his *Laws*, and Aristotle's,

60

in his *Politics*, thus had available as material the whole history of the great days of independent Greece.

Just as Thucydides transmitted his reflections on the greatness of Athens in the fifth century in the form of a funeral oration by Pericles, Plato transmitted his in an account of the trial and death of Socrates. No account of the descent from democracy to demagoguery could be more poignant than Socrates' words:

"There are many reasons why I am not grieved, O men of Athens, at the vote of condemnation. I expected it, and am only surprised that the votes are so nearly equal; for I had thought that the majority against me would have been far larger; but now, had thirty votes gone over to the other side, I should have been acquitted. . . . Perhaps you think that I am braving you in what I am saying now, as in what I said before about the tears and prayers. But this is not so. I speak rather because I am convinced that I never intentionally wronged any one, although I cannot convince you—the time has been too short; if there were a law at Athens, as there is in other cities, that a capital cause should not be decided in one day, then I believe that I should have convinced you. But I cannot in a moment refute great slanders; and, as I am convinced that I never wronged another, I will assuredly not wrong myself. I will not say of myself that I deserve any evil, or propose any remedy. . . . And if I say exile (and this may possibly be the penalty which you will affix), I must indeed be blinded by the love of life, if I am so irrational as to expect that when you, who are my own citizens, cannot endure my discourses and words, and have found them so grievous and odious that you will have no more of them, others are likely to endure me. . . . For I am quite sure that wherever I go, there, as here, the young men will flock to me; and if I drive them away, their elders will drive me out at their request; and if I let them come, their fathers and friends will drive me out for their sakes. . . .

"Not much time will be gained, O Athenians, in return for the evil name which you will get from the detractors of the city, who will say that you killed Socrates, a wise man; for they will call me wise, even although I am not wise, when they want to reproach you. If you had waited a little time, your desire would have been fulfilled in the course of nature. . . .

"But I had not the boldness or impudence or inclination to address you as you would have liked me to do, weeping and wailing and lamenting, and saying and doing many things which you have been accustomed to hear from others, and which, as I maintain, are unworthy of me. . . .

"For neither in war nor yet at law ought I or any man to use every way of escaping death. Often in battle there can be no doubt that if a man will throw away his arms, and fall on his knees before his pursuers, he may escape death; and in other dangers there are other ways of escaping death, if a man is willing to say and do anything. The difficulty, my friends, is not to avoid death, but to avoid unrighteousness; for that runs faster than death. I am old and move slowly, and the slower runner has overtaken me, and my accusers are keen and quick, and the faster runner, who is unrighteousness, has overtaken them. And now I depart hence condemned by you to suffer the penalty of death, —they too go their ways condemned by the truth to suffer the penalty of villainy and wrong; and I must abide by my reward—let them abide by theirs. I suppose that these things may be regarded as fated,—and I think that they are well."

Today, the Agora, the meeting and market place, which housed the government and the daily life of Athens in the age of Pericles, has been uncovered. The area comprises the gently sloping land at the base and to the northwest of the Acropolis. From the steps of the Hephaisteion, itself newly erected about 450 B.C., one can look down on the Agora and see the architectural pattern in which Athenian politics and Athenian philosophy produced this enduring heritage.

To one's left, the north side of the Agora, cut off from the rest by the tracks of the interurban railway from Athens to the Peiraeus, is still

undug. Here was located the Painted Portico, the Stoa Poikile, where followers of the philosopher Zeno gathered; they became known as Stoics.

Similarly, to the east, beyond the opposite end of the Agora, nineteenth century houses still cover areas where interspersed clearings reveal sites dating from Roman times—the market of Caesar and Augustus, the Library of Hadrian, the building known as the Tower of the Winds which was equipped originally with weather vane, sundials, and water clock.

The land below the Hephaisteion served as the Athenian center of public administration at least from the time of Solon, but destruction during the occupation of the city by the Persians required new building when the Athenians regained control. The political monuments of Periclean Athens then took form and continued to be the center of civic life until sacked by the barbarians in A.D. 267.

To provide an administrative headquarters for the city's magistrates, a new Tholos was erected just below the Hephaisteion about 470 B.C. The fifty officials who presided over the meetings of the Council took their meals here.

Beside the Tholos rose the new Bouleuterion, or Council House; its curved tiers of raised seats provided a model for senates everywhere today.

The ruins in front of the Bouleuterion are of a sizable Metroön— temple of the Mother of the gods—that was renewed in the second century B.C. It was used additionally, and in large part, as an archives office for official documents. Previously, two successive senate houses stood upon this site, of which the first went back to Solon's time.

Beyond the Tholos is a building believed to have been the Athenian war office, headquarters of the board of generals, the *strategoi*.

Opposite the Metroön, and on the other side of the Great Drain that leads away the torrents descending from the Acropolis, is the base of a long monument on which stood statues of the legendary Eponymous Heroes, who gave their names to the Attic tribes. The sides of the base of this monument were used as a public bulletin board: citizens who wished to propose new laws at the Assembly had to post them in advance; draft notices for the armed services were also posted here.

South of the monument was the Heliaia, the people's court, where citizens pleaded their own cases before citizen juries numbering 201 to 1501.

Not all of the limits of the Agora can be defined, but one stone that still stands where it was placed about 500 B.C. bears the inscription:

I am the boundary stone of the Agora.

In the classical period, a large space in the center of the Agora was used for public assemblies and festivals. Here were taken the votes of the citizenry by which prominent citizens feared as potential tyrants might be ostracized: in the adjacent museum, the fragments of pottery called *ostraca* used for such votes can be seen, inscribed with names such as Aristides, Themistocles, and Xanthippus, father of Pericles. The museum also has examples of marble allotment machines, and the white balls and the black balls used for the selection or rejection of officials. In Roman times, this area became the site of an odeion; its entrance was supported by colossal statues which remain today and which have earned the building the name of the Stoa of the Giants.

These were the major governmental locations within the Agora; elsewhere around the Acropolis were two others. The Assembly convened on the slope of the hill that lies to the southwest of the Agora, known as the Pnyx—the place where people are packed together. This great open-air theater provided space for up to ten thousand people, though attendance probably seldom exceeded five thousand. Citizens filed in through a single entrance where they could be identified; beginning in Pericles' time, assembly service was rewarded by an honorarium that increased as years went by.

It was here that the art of oratory was practiced over two centuries by Aristides, Themistocles, Pericles, Demosthenes; it was here too that demagoguery received its name. The great platform which one sees today, hewn from the living rock, dates from the time of Demosthenes, in the fourth century B.C. Whether or not as a reminder to speakers, a public sundial was erected on the Pnyx in 433 B.C. Assemblies were also held, later, in the Theater of Dionysus.

South of the Agora, the land rises steeply in the hill called the Areopagus. The name came from the legendary trial there of Ares, accused of killing a son of Poseidon. His successful defense was that the young man had attacked his daughter. This was the seat of the Supreme Court. On a platform at the top of a flight of steps were two stones: one of which—the stone of outrage—was for the plaintiff; the other—the stone of resentment—for the defendant. The judges were chosen for life from among retired archons. Where in earlier times these officials had exercised various executive powers during their one-year terms, in the classical period they functioned chiefly as judiciary officers, eligible subsequently for the supreme judiciary, which also had a vaguer general responsibility as guardian of the constitution and of morals.

The Supreme Court's most famous morals case, in the fourth century, had an unanticipated ending. The courtesan Phryne, mistress of Praxiteles, was brought in because she had posed nude for his statue of Aphrodite. As a climax to her defense, her advocate whipped off her garment. The judges saw no evil.

But other activities than government were carried on in the Agora.

Due honor was paid to the gods. Below the temple of Hephaistos was a large stoa of Zeus, also called the Royal Stoa, with a statue in front of it. Smaller temples and statues dotted the area and many of the buildings contained shrines. The early dramatic contests were held here.

But the function that usually drew people to the Agora was the pursuit of commerce. The great colonnades that bordered the market square on all sides provided sheltered locations for an exchange that included both goods and ideas. Philosophers talked, merchants traded.

At the southeast corner of the Agora was the mint, where the owls of Athena set forth to function somewhat as the pound sterling or the gold standard did in a later trading world. Official weights and measures were kept in the Tholos.

The recent restoration of the stoa put up by King Attalos II of Pergamon in the second century B.C. shows how such structures looked; this one framed the eastern side of the Agora. The spaces which were shops in the original now house a museum of Agora finds.

Contemporary excavation and reconstruction show the form and outline of the Agora buildings; for their appearance when peopled with an excited crowd, one can turn to Aristophanes' *Acharnians* and listen to a countryman named Dicaeopolis. His home was in Acharnai, the largest of the Athenian demes, located near Mount Parnes, some seven miles northwest of Athens.

After Pericles, following a dispute with Megara, had passed laws excluding its citizens from Athenian trade, the Megarians sought help from Sparta. Their army was currently pillaging Acharnaian fields. The countryman is anti-Spartan, but also anti-Pericles for bringing on this ravaging of crops and cutting down of vineyards. He complains:

> *Just make it your own case; suppose the Spartans*
> *Had manned a boat, and landed on your islands,*
> *And stolen a pug puppy from Seriphos;*
> *Would you then have remained at home inglorious?*
> *Not so, by no means; at the first report,*
> *You would have launched at once three hundred gallies,*
> *And filled the city with the noise of troops;*
> *And crews of ships, crowding and clamouring*
> *About the muster-masters and pay-masters;*
> *With measuring corn out at the magazine,*
> *And all the porch choked with the multitude;*
> *With figures of Minerva, newly furbished,*
> *Painted and gilt, parading in the streets;*
> *With wineskins, kegs, and firkins, leeks and onions;*
> *With garlic crammed in pouches, nets, and pokes;*
> *With garlands, singing girls, and bloody noses.*
> *Our arsenal would have sounded and resounded*
> *With bangs and thwacks of driving bolts and nails;*
> *With shaping oars, and holes to put the oar in;*
> *With hacking, hammering, clattering and boring;*
> *Words of command, whistles and pipes and fifes.*
> > *Such would have been your conduct. Will you say,*
> *That Telephus should have acted otherwise?*

Commercial and military activity such as this funneled in and out of the gates at the northwest corner of the city. Various roads converged there; one connected Athens with its harbor outlets on the Aegean.

The city's original anchorages were at Munychia and Phaleron, the places nearest to Athens on the coast. Those harbors still exist: Munychia is today a delightful marina crammed with masted small craft; here, at by no means unreasonable prices, one may rent one of the sturdy boats equipped with motor and sail, called caiques, complete with master and crew and sleeping six to eight passengers, for voyages among the Greek islands or to the Asia Minor shore. Even if not bound for the sea, one can lunch, or better still dine in the cool of the evening, at tables within hawser's length of the gaily painted boats, at any of a score of small restaurants flanking the dockside. Groups who have selected their fish in the interior across the street, sit at the waterside eating fried octopus or cracking toasted pistachio nuts until the main course comes.

But Themistocles expanded Athenian port facilities to include the whole peninsula of the Peiraeus. To the eastern anchorages he added the Main Port to the west, which has a more extensive roadway for larger vessels; he fortified the entire area with stout walls. After his ostracism, Cimon and Pericles completed his work by connecting the defenses of the Peiraeus with those of Athens: high wooden walls were built on each side of the road along the entire six-mile stretch between city and harbor.

The arriving traveler, merchant, athlete, poet, adventurer, philosopher, or king who came into Athens from the west, whether from the Peiraeus, from along the Megara-Corinth road, from Eleusis, or from the nearby grove where Plato had his Academy, approached the city through rows of elaborate monuments to the illustrious or beloved dead, in the Kerameikos Cemetery. Pausanias notes that not far from the gates is a grave, surmounted by a warrior standing beside a horse:

"who he is I know not, but both horse and warrior are by Praxiteles. "When we have entered into the city we come to a building for the

68

getting ready of the processions which are conducted at yearly and other intervals. Hard by is a temple of Demeter with images of the goddess, her daughter and Iacchus, who is holding a torch. An inscription in Attic letters on the wall declares that they are works of Praxiteles. . . . Colonnades run from the gate to the Ceramicus, and in front of them are bronze statues of such men and women as had some title to fame. . . . After the precinct of Dionysus is a building containing images of clay: They represent Amphictyon, king of Athens, feasting Dionysus and other gods. Here too is Pegasus of Eleutherae, who introduced the god to the Athenians. . . . The place called the Ceramicus has its name from a hero Ceramus, said to be a son of Dionysus and Ariadne. . . . Behind is built a colonnade with paintings of the gods who are called the Twelve. On the opposite wall are painted Theseus, Democracy, and the People. The painting signifies that it was Theseus who established political equality at Athens . . ."

The greatest of the processions starting from the Dipylon Gate was the quadrennial Panathenaia, which drew participants from all over Attica. It climaxed four days of contests in music, dancing, and song, and athletic games in the stadium. Old and young, military men and civilians, youths and maidens, horsemen and charioteers were in the long line that traversed the Sacred Way across the Agora, then around and up the steep slopes of the Acropolis, finally across the entrance ramp, into the sacred precinct. The central piece in the procession was a ship on wheels, on whose mast a superbly embroidered peplos, to be dedicated to Athena, served as a symbolic sail.

THE ACROPOLIS

In classical times, the Acropolis, high on its sheer and commanding rock, was solely a scene of religious ceremony.

Earlier, it had been a center of court life and a bastion for defense as well. The legendary kings Erechtheus and Aegeus held it as their citadel.

It was here that Aegeus recognized Theseus, newly come from Troezen, as his heir; it was here too that he watched for the ships of Theseus, returning from his expedition to Crete, and when they came, saw that their sails were black. In fact, Theseus had not been sacrificed to the Minotaur; he had killed the monstrous creature. But he had neglected to change the black sails of his ships to the white ones that were to have signaled a successful mission; stricken with grief, the old king flung himself from this rock and, dying, gave his name to the Aegean.

In historic times, the citadel has likewise served as a defense point, and has witnessed many successive conquerors, from the Persians before the battle of Salamis through the Macedonians, the Romans, the Franks, the Catalans, the Florentines, the Turks, the Venetians, and the Turks again, to the soldiers of Mussolini and Hitler in World War II.

But in the fifth century B.C., the area was set apart as sacred to two rival deities: Athena and Poseidon. They were alleged to have competed before the populace for pre-eminence in the city: Poseidon struck the rock with his trident—one can see the hole today—and a well of salt water appeared, offering control of the seas. Athena struck it with her spear, and an olive tree grew, offering food and wisdom. The people chose the olive tree, and Athena became the city's patron, but Poseidon was likewise venerated. The well remains; the archaeologists have replaced the olive. In the Erechtheion, Athena and Poseidon share honors. But the Parthenon belongs to Athena.

Very shortly after the battle of Salamis, Themistocles made a start on a new Parthenon; but when he was ostracized, work was abandoned. It was under Pericles that a commission whose members were two architects, Iktinos and Kallikrates, and a sculptor, Pheidias, was appointed to start the purifying and rebuilding of the Acropolis that gave it its present form.

Pericles supplied the project with ample funds, in part from the yield of Athenian commerce in such staples as olive oil and wine, in part

70

from the silver mined at Laurion in eastern Attica, in part from overseas spoils and the money paid in by members of the Delian Confederation.

Most materials were close at hand. Far back in prehistory, unknown builders of the Acropolis constructed supporting walls of fitted blocks so huge that inhabitants later called them Cyclopian or Pelasgic—made by giants; the stone was taken from the rocktop itself. Tufa, "poros" stone from the Peiraeus, was used for early buildings; the statues in these temples were wooden images—*xoana*—developed from the sacred trees or pillars of still more primitive days.

71

By the time of Peisistratos, the Athenians were not only gathering the famous honey from the thyme-covered slopes of Mount Hymettos southeast of the city; they were quarrying marble there.

For the Periclean Acropolis, still whiter marble was obtained from Mount Pentelicon, northeast of Athens; black marble from Eleusis— the color is bluish—was introduced for occasional contrast in a dado or a frieze.

The only material which came from any great distance was marble for statuary less brittle than the local varieties; it was imported from Aegean islands such as Naxos and Paros.

The new Acropolis took form rapidly: begun in 447 B.C., the Parthenon was nearly complete within a decade. Remodeling, with Philocles as one of the architects, was started at the Erechtheion in 421 and finished before the end of the century.

Building at the Propylaia, the imposing entrance to the area of the sanctuaries, got under way in 438 under the architect Mnesikles; but the structure was left incomplete after Sparta defeated Athens at the end of the Peloponnesian War.

Entry into the Acropolis still follows the path of the ancient ceremonial processions. The gate below it, called the Beule Gate from the archaeologist who identified it, displays the remains of a much-built-over Roman approach with steps; the ugly pedestal on the left was set up by the princes of Pergamon and re-used to support a chariot group of Agrippa, the son-in-law of the Emperor Augustus.

The structures of the classical period thus start with the Propylaia. On its west side, a Doric colonnade, whose interior is separated into aisles by Ionic columns, fronts the portal. Some of its marble ceiling coffers are in place; through their thin translucent central layers, unroofed today, comes a lovely light. To the left is a room which was a picture gallery. To the right of the Sacred Way is an outward-projecting bastion with a small temple to Athena Nike, also called Athena

Apteros, the wingless Victory—at the height of their power, Athenians said she was wingless because she would never need to fly away.

The two portals on either side of the main entrance of the Propylaia are reached by steps; the processional ramp goes through the central opening.

Once inside, and after that moment when he catches his breath at the realization that he is really there, the visitor has two choices.

As a student, he can view the two great buildings, the Parthenon and

74

the Erechtheion, in detail; find the highest point of the Acropolis where stood the altar of Zeus, locate the site of the pedestal from which Pheidias' gleaming bronze statue of Athena Promachos, thirty feet high, reflected sunlight to lookouts far out at sea.

In equal detail, in the museum at the far end of the rock, he can study statues and friezes that were on the Acropolis buildings of the seventh and sixth centuries, together with fragments from the Parthenon and the Nike Temple—from the frieze of the latter the relief of the goddess untying her sandal.

Herakles makes three appearances: being presented by Iris to Zeus and Athena; killing the Hydra while a crab sent by Hera to help the Hydra bites his foot; fighting a Triton, with the fight watched by the sea-monster Typhon, which has three heads of bearded men and a

triple-coiled snake's body. Lions fight bulls; men fight giants. The polychrome of the original paint is still on many of the contours.

These are all pieces from either pediments or friezes. Separate statues include a collection of *Korai*—damsels—wearing marvelous chitons with embroidered skirts held up by the ladies' left hands, embroidered shawls fastened at the right shoulder and draped under the other arm, elaborate hairdress and diadems. While the clothing has many variations, the faces all exhibit the same forced, archaic smile—did the Greeks have a

word for "cheese"? Other statues include a man carrying a calf across his shoulders and a fine, lithe dog.

In the Parthenon, the student can redecipher the original floor plan, see the spot where Pheidias' chryselephantine statue of Athena was dedicated at the Panathenaic festival of 438 B.C. This masterwork was nearly forty feet tall; the eyes were inlaid with semiprecious stones, the body covered with a garment of gold plates. Pheidias made the plates so they were removable; when gossip accused him of stealing some of

the gold, it is said that he took off the plates and weighed them in vindication. Later, vandals simply took them off.

Outside, the informed observer can note the eight columns at each end, the seventeen on each side, that exemplify the classic formula that the long side of a temple should have twice as many columns as the ends, plus one. He can note the slight convex curve of the steps that lead up to the stylobate and the slight inward incline of the columns; together, these variations turn what would have been the rigidity of rectilinear rectitude into graciousness that seems almost without weight.

He can note the parts of the frieze and the figures on the pediments that remain in place, observing the adaptations of the frieze to accord with the low position from which it is viewed, and the accommodation of the statues to the exigencies of the triangular shape of the pediments.

The Erechtheion exemplifies the architectural problem of designing a new building without violating traditional locations and traditional reverence. This site, unlike that of the Parthenon, had been long consecrated to a number of deities.

Worship went back to the period when the Earth Goddess and the sacred serpent were revered by peoples who inhabited the Greek peninsula before migrants from the north imported the Olympian theogony. The hero-king Erechtheus—or was it the serpent-boy named Erichthonios—was venerated here. Poseidon had his portico, and a thunderbolt of Zeus its place. In the old shrine of Athena was a primitive statue of olive wood, a religious object whereas Pheidias' masterpiece was a work of art.

No attempt was made to superimpose a unified plan upon this variety; the architect simply decorated the oddly-shaped building that housed all this tradition with all the skill at his command.

The capitals and bases of the Ionic columns of the portico that lead to Poseidon's precinct are adorned with finest detail; elaborate carving frames his entrance door.

79

The porch facing the Parthenon is supported by six *korai* or caryatids in place of pillars—today, one of the six is actually a cast, replacing the original in the British Museum, and one is much repaired.

The frieze of the Erechtheion, like the dadoes, steps, and trim of the Propylaia, instances the use of Eleusinian black marble to contrast with white.

Starting with such initial observations, the student can go deeper and deeper into history, legend, archaeology.

But the visitor does not have to remain always a student. There is another way to see the Acropolis. He can come as an artist, freed of the details of dates, sequences, relationships, and feel it with his senses rather than examine it with his mind.

He can look at columns outlined in vibrant light against the intense blue of the midday sky.

Through long-shadowed portals he can watch the sun drop behind Mount Aegaleos where Xerxes watched the light fade on the battle of Salamis, remaining until the dusk from the sea engulfs plain and city in a purple afterglow.

And on each night of full moon, or the night before or after, when the Acropolis is open until midnight, he can see it as blue light and black background, form almost without substance, undistracted by the incidents of the day.

In the moonlight, even though there may be many people, voices are hushed. Movement becomes shadow.

Where sunlight is diffuse, moonlight is selective. Where sunlight emphasizes the mellow yellowing of time, moonlight blues it out, to create pristine white again.

By day, the very human pluralism of the Erechtheion attracts affection. By night, the beholder turns to the abstract and unified perfection of the Parthenon, experiencing it angle by angle, hour by hour, angle by hour, moving silently, melded with the sentient stone.

CHAPTER 4

When First Nights
Were First Days

MANY of the masterpieces of classic
drama were first performed on the southeast slope of the Acropolis,
where, after some twenty-four hundred years, they may be seen again
today.

To the Greeks, a theater meant an area for presentations in the open
air; an odeion, a covered, all-weather building originally used for choral
concerts and hence known as a music hall.

Pericles built an odeion, of which traces still remain; the later and
better-known example is on a different site. It was given to the city in
the time of the Roman Empire—A.D. 161, to be precise—as a memorial

to his wife Regilla by the munificent Herodes Atticus, who governed a large part of Greece on behalf of Rome, and whose private public works program embellished most of the country's major centers.

The Theater of Dionysus, built for the most part in the fourth century B.C., has retained its original site. Its tiers of ordinary seats are of stone; its ceremonial front rows—seats of the mighty—were constructed in marble after the Periclean period; further adornment, including the reliefs supporting a Roman stage and illustrating the life of Dionysus, dates from Nero's time and later. But in an earlier and simpler setting, this is where many of the great Greek tragedies and comedies had their first days.

Greek drama, tragedy and comedy alike, grew out of the rites of Dionysus. The Boieotians introduced this god of wine and song to the Athenians; his boon companions were Pan and the satyrs. The animal most frequently sacrificed to him was the goat—tragedy means "goat-song."

Two annual festivals began to be held in his honor, one in winter when the new wine was ready to drink, one in spring when nature's fecundity was at its height. Until the fourth century the former, called the Lenean festival—possibly because the *lenos* or wine press was thought to have been invented by Dionysus—was celebrated on the slope between the Areopagus and the Acropolis.

The major festival, in the spring, known as the City Dionysia, was first held near the Agora, but after the temporary wooden seats there collapsed early in the fifth century, the celebration was moved to what became its permanent site.

Before the altar of Dionysus, stories of his life were sung as choral odes. Eventually, the leader of the chorus detached himself to make an explanation of the plot—the prologue—then changed from a commentator to a participant, representing individual characters. Shortly, a second member began to speak parts; subsequently a third and fourth—and the dramatis personae of tragedy were at hand.

Comedy developed from the *komos*, or revel, that took place probably on the evening of the first day of the City Dionysia; revelers—as can be seen from the designs on many Greek vases—sometimes costumed as animals, sometimes performing phallic rites, danced and sang and traded cracks with bystanders.

As the Greek sense of man and destiny deepened, the dramatic festivals came to have less the character of religious ritual. Tales from mythology and the heroic age replaced the life of Dionysus as exclusive subject matter. The form in which the story was presented ceased to be a recital in the third person by a chorus all of whose members were alike. Individualized representation of an awesome human event, with speech in the first and second persons, was combined with commentary in which the chorus applied to the event the wisdom of the community.

Yet over the years, the physical surroundings of actors and chorus are little changed. A central stone representing Dionysus' altar continues to be present. The circular orchestra provides an area in which the chorus performs its chants and measured movements. The audience sits on tiers cut into the side of the hill around some three-fifths of the periphery of the orchestra.

The emergence of actors as persons with parts representing characters is paralleled by the use of costumes and props; a *skene,* or tent, put up back of the orchestra, gives them a place to change; as time goes on, the tent is replaced by a building, usually with three doors for entrances and exits; a proscenium, an area—eventually raised—in front of the scene, gives the actors a place to walk. Behind the scene is located the apparatus by which an actor representing a god can be brought onto the scene from the air—the *deus ex machina.*

During classical times, the Greek theater retained a completely round orchestra; in the Roman period, in theater and odeion alike, the circle was flattened on one side by the moving forward of the proscenium and the scene building.

Particularly because the actors spoke through masks, the acoustics of Greek theaters were centrally important. Audiences everywhere numbered in at least four figures; contemporary estimates of the seating capacity of the Athenian theater ranged from fourteen to thirty thousand.

When First Nights Were First Days

From at least 535 B.C., when the actor-author Thespis had an entry in the competition, there were regular annual dramatic contests in Athens as part of the Greater Dionysia.

The six-day spring ceremony began with a procession; next day a contest was scheduled among ten presentations of dithyrambs, choral odes pertaining to Dionysus and performed by choruses of fifty. Comic drama, with five contestants, was acted on the third day. The last three days were given to tragedy: three poets each offered a tetralogy, usually a trilogy of three dramas on a related subject, plus a satyr-play as an afterpiece.

Since the plays were given as public spectacles, a patron had to be found to bear the expenses of production. In each tribe, a wealthy citizen was designated by the government to serve as *choregos* or producer for one of the various choruses or plays; a dramatist's chances were therefore partly dependent on the generosity with which his sponsor undertook this public service. As recompense, the choregoi of the winning productions received tripods which were then mounted on pedestals as public monuments. The monument of Lysicrates, who sponsored a successful boys' chorus in 334 B.C., exists today—its columns display one of the earliest remaining examples of the Corinthian capital. Usually, authors acted in their plays, though Sophocles is said to have had to forego taking part because of a weak voice.

Fifth century tragedy was successively illuminated by the three great names of Aeschylus, Sophocles, and Euripides. The lives of the three overlapped: Aeschylus fought as a soldier at Salamis; Sophocles is said to have sung in the boys' chorus that celebrated the victory; Euripides had just been born on the island from which the battle took its name. All of them were enormously prolific—since with rare exceptions a play had only one Athenian performance, they had to be.

Aeschylus wrote some eighty plays, of which complete texts of seven are now known; he had his first production in Athens in 499, won the contest for tragedy for the first time in 484, was successful twelve times thereafter.

Sophocles produced some hundred-and-twenty-odd works, of which again seven survive; he defeated Aeschylus with his *Triptolemus* at the festival of 468; but Aeschylus came back the following year with his *Seven Against Thebes*.

The texts of Euripides have been more fortunate: of ninety-two, nineteen remain. His first performance was in 455; his first victory in 442. Yet of the twenty-two competitions in which he engaged, Euripides won only four: in 431, the judges put his *Medea* at the bottom of the list.

Mutual respect among competing tragedians is instanced by the story that Sophocles produced his entry at the festival of 406, the year of his death, with the chorus ungarlanded, in mourning for Euripides, who had died shortly before. Such solidarity among the tragic fraternity may have been strengthened, during the last quarter of the fifth century, by the unlimited ribbing to which their loftinesses were subjected at the very festivals where their works were performed. By this time, the comic contest was no longer held on a separate day; the program provided tragedy in the morning, comedy in the afternoon. The change gave exceptional opportunity to the rising comedian Aristophanes, eleven of whose texts survive. For forty years after his first production in 427, his bold, blunt, bawdy works spared neither institutions nor individuals. As the waning of the political fortunes of the Athenian state stifled criticism of the government, the political satire of his earlier plays—the *Acharnians, Clouds, Wasps,* and *Peace*—turns into the social satire of his *Birds, Lysistrata, Frogs;* but this jester's thwacking bladder was tempted again and again by the masks with the down-turned mouths.

In the *Frogs*, with which Aristophanes won the prize at the Lenean festival of 405, Dionysus is portrayed as being so grieved at the recent death of Euripides that he descends into the realm of Hades to bring him back. Once there, however, he conducts a contest between Aeschylus and Euripides, which surprisingly ends with Aeschylus the victor:

"DIONYSUS: Do you consent to the trial, Aeschylus? Speak.

AESCHYLUS: I might well take objection to the place;
    It's no fair field for him and me.

DIONYSUS: Why not?

AESCHYLUS: Because my writings haven't died with me,
    As his have, so he'll have them all to hand . . .
    However, I waive the point, if you think fit."

Later on, as the contest continues, Euripides protests:

"EURIPIDES: . . . I write my prologues singularly well!

AESCHYLUS: By Zeus, I won't go pecking word by word
    At every little phrase; I'll take one little oil-can,
    God helping me, and send your prologues pop! . . .

DIONYSUS: Begin to quote.

EURIPIDES: "Aegyptus, so the tale is spread afar.
    With fifty youths fled in a sea-borne car,
    But, reaching Argos . . ."

AESCHYLUS: Found his oil-can gone!

DIONYSUS: What's that about the oil-can! Drat the thing!
    Quote him another prologue, and let's see.

EURIPIDES: "Dionysus, who with wand and fawn-skin dight
    On great Parnassus races to the light
    Of lamps far-flashing . . ."

AESCHYLUS: Found his oil-can gone!"

87

The contest ends with the chorus singing:

> *O blessed are they who possess*
> *An extra share of brains!*
> *'Tis a fact that more or less*
> *All fortunes of men express;*
> *As now, by showing*
> *An intellect glowing,*
> *This man his home regains;*
> *Brings benefit far and near*
> *To all who may hold him dear,*
> *And staunches his country's tear,—*
> *All because of his brains!*

The tragedians were, indeed, circumscribed in their art form as other creative artists of the fifth and fourth centuries were not. In architecture and sculpture, in philosophy and science, and in all probability in the lost arts of music and painting as well, new forms burgeoned from new freedom. But partly because of their origin in ritual, dramatic conventions had a set form which, though it might be modified, was nevertheless generally observed.

Similarly, the great tragic plots were already established, and known to the spectators, in advance, by heart. The calamities of the royal houses of Thebes—the Oedipus story—and of Mycenae—the curse on the Atreides—epitomized tragedy and lent themselves to trilogy; all the great dramatists used them. But the changes over time in the way these stories were treated reflect the emergence in fifth century Athens of an awareness of the inner life of the individual, and of a philosophy of man.

In Aeschylus' *Agamemnon*, the Argive Elders describe the inexorable and rough-shod march of fate over his characters' lives:

When First Nights Were First Days

Yet it is true: the high strength of men
knows no content with limitation. Sickness
chambered beside it beats at the wall between.
Man's fate that sets a true
course yet may strike upon
the blind and sudden reefs of disaster.
But if before such time, fear
throw overboard some precious thing
of the cargo, with deliberate cast,
not all the house, laboring
with weight of ruin, shall go down,
nor sink the hull deep within the sea.
And great and affluent the gift of Zeus
in yield of ploughed acres year on year
makes void again sick starvation.

But when the black and mortal blood of man
has fallen to the ground before his feet, who then
can sing spells to call it back again?
Did Zeus not warn us once
when he struck to impotence
that one who could in truth charm back the dead men?
Had the gods not so ordained
that fate should stand against fate
to check any man's excess,
my heart now would have outrun speech
to break forth the water of its grief.
But this is so; I murmur deep in darkness
sore at heart; my hope is gone now
ever again to unwind some crucial good
from the flames about my heart.

In Sophocles' *Antigone*, by contrast, the human spirit is freer: his chorus sings:

"Wonders are many, and none is more wonderful than man; the power that crosses the white sea, driven by the stormy southwind, making a path under surges that threaten to engulf him; and Earth, the eldest of the gods, the immortal, the unwearied, doth he wear, turning the soil with the offspring of horses, as the ploughs go to and fro from year to year.

"And the light-hearted race of birds, and the tribes of savage beasts, and the sea-brood of the deep, he snares in the meshes of his woven toils, he leads captive, man excellent in wit. And he masters by his arts the beast whose lair is in the wilds, who roams the hills; he tames the horse of shaggy mane, he puts the yoke upon its neck, he tames the tireless mountain bull.

"And speech, and wind-swift thought, and all the moods that mould a state, hath he taught himself; and how to flee the arrows of the frost, when 'tis hard lodging under the clear sky, and the arrows of the rushing rain; yea, he hath resource for all; without resource he meets nothing that must come; only against Death shall he call for aid in vain; but from baffling maladies he hath devised escapes.

"Cunning beyond fancy's dream is the fertile skill which brings him, now to evil, now to good. When he honours the laws of the land, and that justice which he hath sworn by the gods to uphold, proudly stands his city: no city hath he who, for his rashness, dwells with sin. Never may he share my hearth, never think my thoughts who doth these things!"

Many of Euripides' choruses are similarly lyrical, as in his *Medea* when the Corinthian women chant:

> *The sons of Erechtheus, the olden,*
> *Whom high gods planted of yore*

When First Nights Were First Days

In an old land of heaven upholden,
   A proud land untrodden of war:
They are hungered, and, lo, their desire
   With wisdom is fed as with meat:
In their skies is a shining of fire,
   A joy in the fall of their feet:
And thither, with manifold dowers,
   From the North, from the hills, from the morn,
The Muses did gather their powers,
   That a child of the Nine should be born,
And Harmony, sown as the flowers,
   Grew gold in the acres of corn.

But it is quite unnecessary to be content with reading, or reading about, these dramas of twenty-four hundred years ago. One can see them re-enacted today, their current first nights within sight of the scene of their original first days. On the slope of the Acropolis, where the Theater of Dionysus itself is being restored, the Odeion of Herodes Atticus currently houses the long season of the Athenian summer festival. This includes presentations of modern drama and ballet, frequently by visiting companies from other countries, but the visitor can be assured of a chance to see a variety of classical plays given in Greek, and the size of the Odeion, though it is usually well filled, offers him a reasonable chance of obtaining tickets.

Today, women's parts are taken by women, and the actors do not wear masks, but the performances are otherwise in classic form. The chorus, whether cast as the writhing Furies in *The Eumenides*, the daughters of Oceanus in *Prometheus Bound*, the elders of Thebes in *Oedipus the King*, or the frogs in Aristophanes' comedy of that name, executes its stylized chant and dance. When appearing as Theban elders, two of the chorus are indubitably personages whom one has seen elsewhere, statues come to life. The group is costumed in gray material that hangs in folds as heavy as if they were of stone. One of its members is certainly the charioteer of Delphi: his body is straight, calm, intense; in his bronze face the cornea of his eyes are white as the stone insets in antique statues. Another figure is elongated in every line: fingers, body, beard. He, equally obviously, is on temporary leave from his usual position as one of the archaic kings of the west portal of Chartres Cathedral.

Unexpected events in these current dramatic presentations can likewise recall the past. In the summer of 1959, Aristophanes' *Birds* was produced in Athens. On its first night, an angry and explosive audience booed it to permanent withdrawal on the ground that the producer's presentation óf the pagan priest resembled a priest of the Orthodox church. Twenty-four hundred years earlier, Aeschylus had a like experience. His native city was nearby Eleusis, the shrine of the Eleusinian Mysteries. All Athenians were initiated into at least the first degree of these mysteries. In the course of a play in which he was acting, a reference to Demeter gave the audience the impression that Aeschylus had revealed a secret. Wrathful spectators rose in the stands, poured down into the orchestra. Aeschylus found temporary safety by hastening to take sanctuary at the altar of Dionysus. Thereafter, charged before the Areopagus with a breach of security, he testified he did not know that what he said constituted revelation of classified material, and obtained an acquittal. Gossips, however, credited the success of his defense rather to the military standing which he and his brother shared as veterans of Marathon—they were among the heroes portrayed in the frescoes of the Painted Stoa in the Agora.

Classic plays and traditional dances may also be seen today in places other than Athens. In the ancient theater beside the museum at the Peiraeus, groups from many provinces of Greece present local folk dances in costume.

These too, frequently portray old stories, like the dance from Epirus which commemorates the mass suicide of the women of the beleaguered mountain village of Suli above Parga. Inaccessible though the place is, the Turks were about to take it. Rather than fall into their hands, the women danced a dance with a winding motif like the endless spinning of wool in this sheep-herding area; as each one reached the end of the figure, she wound herself off the cliff.

Other dances are based on the boy-meets-girl motif; in the *ballos* the boy and girl put more provocation into two whirling handkerchiefs than is obtainable in the west without far greater exposure.

Still others are shepherd dances, such as the breathlessly vigorous *pentozali* of Crete.

Among the most ancient is the dance of the cranes, the *geranos*, said to go back to the time of Theseus.

A further theatrical festival, held in the Peloponnese in early June, is at Epidauros, southeast of Corinth near the Argive coast. The theater there is the most perfect that now exists; it was designed in the latter part of the fourth century B.C. by Polyclitus the Younger. The orchestra preserves its perfect circle. Stone seats for fourteen thousand spectators are cut out of a foothill of Mount Cynortium; the ordinary benches are of white limestone, the special front row seats, of pink. The tiers of seats rise to a vertical height of 74 feet above the level of the orchestra; their radius at this point is some 193 feet.

Yet the acoustics are so perfect that even when the theater is empty, a breath of sound can be heard everywhere.

When I was seventeen, I studied ancient Greek. In the winter, it was by the usual means, grammar, dictionary, composition, long drill on irregular verbs. But in summer, it was different. Walter Bridgman used to take me fishing, in his rowboat, on a pine-and-birch surrounded Michigan lake. He knew most of the *Iliad* and the *Odyssey* by heart. As the water patted the anchored bow, he used to recite long sequences; forty years later, I know them still.

Such transmission of a tradition is surely a human form of immor-

tality; Walter Bridgman, who never saw Greece, has been dead for many years.

So, thinking of him at Epidauros, after the strangers had left the theater, I went to the stone at the center of the orchestra and recited the lines from the end of the eighth book of the *Iliad* that like the scene before battle in Shakespeare's *Henry* V recount the silences of men who wait upon the bridges of war.

οἱ δὲ μέγα φρονέοντες ἐπὶ πτολέμοιο γεφύρας
ἥατο παννύχιοι, πυρὰ δέ σφισι καίετο πολλά.
ὡς δ' ὅτ' ἐν οὐρανῷ ἄστρα φαεινὴν ἀμφὶ σελήνην
φαίνετ' ἀριπρεπέα, ὅτε τ' ἔπλετο νήνεμος αἰθήρ·
ἔκ τ' ἔφανεν πᾶσαι σκοπιαὶ καὶ πρώονες ἄκροι
καὶ νάπαι· οὐρανόθεν δ' ἄρ' ὑπερράγη ἄσπετος αἰθήρ,
πάντα δὲ εἴδεται ἄστρα, γέγηθε δέ τε φρένα ποιμήν·
τόσσα μεσηγὺ νεῶν ἠδὲ Ξάνθοιο ῥοάων
Τρώων καιόντων πυρὰ φαίνετο Ἰλιόθι πρό.
χίλι' ἄρ' ἐν πεδίῳ πυρὰ καίετο, πὰρ δὲ ἑκάστῳ
ἥατο πεντήκοντα σέλα πυρὸς αἰθομένοιο.
ἵπποι δὲ κρῖ λευκὸν ἐρεπτόμενοι καὶ ὀλύρας
ἑσταότες παρ' ὄχεσφιν ἐΰθρονον Ἠῶ μίμνον.

And above me, the words were audible in the topmost tier.

CHAPTER 5 *Cape Sounion and the Sea*

IN Greece, the land matters less than the sea.
By and large, the land is harsh and grudging. There are the fertile
plains of Thrace and Thessaly, the arable acres of Boieotia, the lowlands
of the west coast. In the Peloponnese, there are the rich valleys of the
Eurotas and the Pamisos and the fruited plain of Argos. Where there
is water, the soil yields graciously; where fields are level, there is abun-
dance. But there is little water, and little level land.

Even in ancient times, the ax and the plow had bared the surface;
the rains came, and it washed away. Pausanias writes of the valley of the
Maeander that "because it was ploughed on both banks, the silt had
made solid land out of the sea around Miletus." Over millennia, and

97

in our own time, war after war has exacerbated deforestation. There are still pine forests in the north around Mount Olympus to the east and near the Katara Pass to the west, whose living needles soften the wind and whose fallen needles mitigate the rain, but they stand almost alone as natural cover. Elsewhere, the Greek landscape is mostly a terrain of stones.

On the mountain sides, stone walls separate but hardly differentiate the fields from their boundaries. In search of wisps, erect-tailed goats trifle with gravity at angles seeming only minutes removed from ninety degrees; in sight of their wandering appetites, reforestation requires the placement of six-foot triangular wooden barricades around each seedling. Even on less precipitous slopes where sheep as well as goats are grazed, whatever is green is rooted up, leaving loose dust amid the gravel.

From this harsh land, the Greeks followed the fertility out to sea, first to where the fish were feeding, then into the channels of Aegean and Mediterranean commerce.

The sea too is harsh: many epitaphs in the *Greek Anthology* witness its cruelty and its toll. Plato is thought to have written that which reads:

> *Here is a sailor's tomb: there lies*
> *A tiller of the soil:*
> *Death comes alike on sea and land*
> *To those who toil.*

Antipater mourned:

"Even in death shall the unappeased sea vex me, Lysis, buried as I am beneath this desert rock, sounding ever harshly in my ears close to my deaf tomb. Why, O men, did ye lay me next to her who reft me of breath, who wrecked me not trading on a merchantman, but embarked

on a little rowing boat? From the sea I sought to gain my living, and from the sea I drew forth death."

Glaucus of Nicopolis said:

"Not this earth or this light stone that rests thereon is the tomb of Erasippus, but all this sea whereon thou lookest. For he perished along with his ship, and his bones are rotting somewhere, but where only the gulls can tell."

Yet the mariners persisted. Theodoridaes writes:

"I am the tomb of a shipwrecked man; but set sail, stranger; for when we were lost, the other ships voyaged on."

Cape Sounion and the Sea

There came early into the eyes of the Greeks the wary look of sailors everywhere who pit their skills against the changeable violence of the sea.

The Aegean's willfulness has multiple causes. The depth of the sea floor varies greatly: in many places, its basin is the counterpart of the shallow lakes that exist in several parts of mainland Greece, with a depth of only two or three hundred feet; elsewhere fissures open in the ocean floor, again like the clefts of the Greek mountains, to drop several thousand feet.

The multitude of islands and peninsulas, of rocks that break the surface, and of shoals that lurk below it, gives rise to powerful currents within the sea that can speed or smash small craft running straits or rounding capes.

Main currents move north to south in the central Aegean, curl back close to its shores. The winds vary with the seasons: strong south-to-north winds churn the waters in winter; even the Etesian winds out of the northeast in the summer months, which cool the islands and which used to speed home the annual wheat and fish fleets from the Black Sea, are often strong enough to raise sudden whitecaps under a clear sky.

The skill of the mariner is to know these things and to profit by them. Hesiod, in his *Works and Days* gives counsel to his brother:

> As for you, Perses, remember the timely seasons
>   for all work
> done, but remember it particularly about seafaring.
> Admire a little ship, but put your cargo in a big one.
> The bigger the cargo, the bigger will be
>   the profit added
> to profit—if only the winds hold off
>   their harsh gales from it.

But for when, turning your easily blown thoughts
    toward a merchant's
life, you wish to escape your debts,
    and unhappy hunger,
I will show you the measures
    of the much-thundering sea, I
who am not one who has much knowledge of ships
    and sea-voyages;
for I never did sail in a ship across the wide water
except across to Euboia from Aulis, where once
        the Achaians
stayed out the storm and gathered together
    a great many people
from sacred Hellas to go to Troy
    the land of fair women.

This is all my experience with intricately bolted
ships, but I can still tell you the thought,
    which is of aegis-bearing
Zeus, for the muses have taught me to sing
    immortal poetry.
    For fifty days after the turn
    of the summer solstice,
when the wearisome season of the hot weather
    goes to its conclusion
then is the timely season for me to voyage.
    You will not
break up your ship, nor will the sea drown
    its people, unless
Poseidon, the shaker of the earth,
    of his own volition,

Cape Sounion and the Sea

or Zeus, the king of the immortals, wishes
    to destroy it,
for with these rests authority for all outcomes,
    good or evil.

At that time the breezes can be judged,
    and the sea is untroubled.
At that time, trusting your swift ship to the winds,
    you can draw her
down to the sea at will, and load all your cargo
    inside her;
but make haste still, for the sake of
    an earlier home-coming,
and do not wait for the season of the new wine,
    and the autumn
rain, and the winter coming on,
    and the hard-blowing southwind
who comes up behind the heavy rains that Zeus sends
    in autumn
and upheaves the sea and makes the open water
    difficult.
        There is one other sailing season for men,
    in spring time.
At that point, when you first make out
    on topmost branches
of the fig tree, a leaf as big as the print
    that a crow makes
when he walks; at that time also the sea is navigable
and this is called the spring sailing season.
    I for my part
do not like it. There is nothing about it
    that I find pleasant.
It's snatched.

Cape Sounion and the Sea

Against Hesiod's testimony on the spring season, however, must be set the lyric of Leonidas in the *Greek Anthology:*

"This is the season for sailing. For the twittering swallow has already come, and the pleasant Zephyrs; and the meadows are in flower, and silent has become the sea, broken (lately) by waves and rough gales. Take up the anchors, sailor, and let loose the ropes, and set sail, giving out the whole canvass. This do I, Priapus, enjoin, who inhabit the harbour, in order that you, O man, may set sail for every kind of traffic."

Many a Greek sailor's destination can be seen in a single sweep from the sharp headland of the southeast tip of Attica, at Cape Sounion. To the west, with the little island of Patroclus in the near foreground, the coast recedes toward the Peiraeus and Athens, toward Aegina, Hydra, and the other islands of the Saronic Gulf, with the Peloponnese behind them. Straight south, the way lies clear to Crete. To the east, beyond close-lying Makronisos, is Kea, westernmost island of the Cyclades. Euboia lies off the cape around its eastern point.

Far below the brown cliff, upon the crinkled surface of the purple sea, little ships, dwarfed by distance, ply these lanes of commerce. Blue snake currents toil and turn athwart their courses.

From at least the sixth century B.C., the point at Sounion has been dedicated to a god. In early times, it was Athena Sounias; the ruin of her temple has been identified. But in the great age of Greece, under Pericles, when the Hephaisteion and the Parthenon were new, the height was consecrated with a magnificent temple of white marble, honoring Poseidon, the sea-god who both causes and quells the tempest.

Twelve twenty-foot columns and an architrave are in place; from close to twenty miles out at sea their gleaming surface can be distinguished from the duller color of the cliff.

At Sounion, I was rewarded for recalcitrance.

I had come out from Athens with a group of people, and other groups of people were there when we arrived. I wanted to see Sounion alone.

At the refreshment area some rods away, I asked the French-speaking proprietor if he could communicate with the little hotel which is about a mile and a half down in the protected cove, and find me lodging for the night.

For some time I sat at the cliff-side and watched a small boat come closer until its crew became distinguishable, turned into individuals, and, as they chugged by the cliff's base, held up their caps to hail the craning visitors.

The proprietor returned, sadly. All rooms were full.

My response was a prolonged, sodden, and histrionic silence. He stood. Then, with the key word spoken in italics, he said he supposed madame would not be interested in "une chambre *absolument* sans confort?"

I took it like a trout on the rise. I confirmed a full understanding and acceptance of what "absolutely without comfort" might mean; I asked him to tell his friends that I would look forward to taking dinner at the hotel; I ascertained that the workmen employed on the current excavation below the temple would be up and about and the gate in the wired-off enclosure consequently open, not too long after sunup. I surprised my Athenian bus conductor with a request to count me out on the return journey. Little bag in hand (I had been forethoughtful), I set off down the hill.

The hotel has a lighted balcony just wide enough for a single row of tables, facing the headland and the sea. With the leisurely meal went a sweet and general fragrance from thriving boxes of petunias on the ledge, and a sharp and concentrated scent from the retsina wine.

A childhood partly spent in the upper branches of pine trees, where balls of chewy resin welling from woodpecker holes were regarded as a happy find, had prepared me fully for the resinated wines of Greece.

Cape Sounion and the Sea

The thyrsos of Dionysus is twined with vine, topped with a pine cone, and the wine of the country, likewise, combines the fruit of the vine with the resin of the pine. For a special evening, the unresinated Greek wines—Rhodos, Minos, Demestika—are perhaps preferable, but taken as a wholly different sort of drink, particularly in very hot weather, retsina has its pleasures.

After a time, I looked up my host, announced that I was wholly ready for the room *"absolument sans confort."*

He called his son. The youngster took my little bag, scampered out the back door, sped with goatlike agility up the hill. I scrambled after him; it was a night of nearly full moon.

He mounted past one or two cottages where people sitting in the dooryards called a greeting, then turned still farther up, across stony ground.

We came to a low dark structure, with two doors. The lad pushed open one of them, set down the little bag, proudly flicked on a light bulb hanging from its wire. The space contained a single iron bed. I thanked him. Wheeling, again goatlike, he was gone.

Over dinner, I had planned what I actually did the next morning: the walk through the early light, the climb to the top of the cliff, the solitude which Byron apostrophized in his *Isles of Greece:*

> *Place me on Sunium's marbled steep,*
> > *Where nothing, save the waves and I,*
> > *May hear our mutual murmurs sweep. . . .*

At the monument, I would observe angles of white and black, high column and long shadow; after I had a feel for their patterns, I would carefully compose photographs, without rushing the click of the shutter to avoid including either bearded-student-and-pony-tailed-friend, or the fat-and-foot-hurting-group-from-the-woman's-club. I would listen to the silence of the sea.

In due course, I would return to breakfast on the hotel terrace, then

jounce to Athens in the local bus that starts as though its destination were Marathon; as human compression increased from stop to stop, I would hold people's children and parcels on my lap. And that is what happened.

But that night, I had a prior experience. Once in a while, an unexpected, breath-taking by-product, attained in the course of pursuing another purpose, becomes far more significant than one's original plan. There on the mountain side I cut the light and turned to the door of the cabin, half guessing—but only half—what I would see.

I was higher than the headland. Down the slope, the lights of the cluster of houses around the hotel were to the left, out of the way of the central vista. In front of me, the darkness of the land was unbroken until it touched the sea. Across the crinkled water, the silver wake of the moon lay wide to the west. On the crest of the headland, the moonlit marble of the temple was faintly luminous.

Until the wake dwindled, time was measured only by the beating of my heart.

CHAPTER 6 *Delos: Center of Trade*

PATRONAGE of a god, commerce of men, a
location at the center of the Aegean and Eastern Mediterranean worlds
combined to change the island of Delos from a barren rock three miles
long and not quite one mile wide to the site of a magnificent city whose
ruins, inhabited now only by the quick lizard and the shy finch, still
take half a day to traverse.

The god was Apollo. His birthplace was provided by his aunt.
Amorous Zeus, in one of his many pursuits, had followed the unwilling
maiden Asteria; to escape him, she changed herself into a quail and
dropped into the sea, where she became an island that floated over
the waters, *a-delos*, invisible.

With Asteria's sister Leto, Zeus was more successful; as her time for delivery approached, Leto sought a place where she might escape the wrath of Zeus' disapproving consort, Hera. Asteria consented to harbor her.

Leto gave birth to twins: Artemis, born with no difficulty, promptly aided her mother in her further labor, which lasted for nine days. Then, clinging to a palm tree, with Zeus observing pleasurably from the height of the island's conical peak, Mount Cynthos, Leto gave birth to Apollo. Ecstatic Zeus ordered Poseidon to anchor the floating island to the bottom of the sea with adamantine pillars: thereafter, Delos was visible.

So from the earliest times, the shrine of Apollo on Delos was a magnet for wealth, votive offerings, ceremony, delegations from a distance, through all the lands of Greece.

In the later years of prehistory, the Cyclades, among which Delos is the central island, were occupied by the Ionian people. Naxos, as early as the seventh century, sent major offerings to the Delian shrine; in the sixth century, Polycrates of Samos made a gift of the island of Rheneia, which lies so close that his present could be attached to Delos by a symbolic chain.

But the rise of Delos did not go unobserved in Athens.

As recorded in legend, Theseus, heir of Aegeus, king of Athens, stopped at Delos on his return from vanquishing the Minotaur in Crete, instituted the dance of the *geranos* around the shrine of Artemis, and founded the Delian Games, whose victors were crowned with palms in memory of the tree to which Leto clung.

As recorded in history, on the strength of a common Ionian ancestry, Athens took increasing interest in the affairs of the Ionian islands and in 477 B.C., after Salamis, established a new structure to unite their maritime strength under Athenian hegemony against future invasion. The Athenian hegemony developed into empire; Pericles took over the Delian Treasury.

Delos: Center of Trade

However, it appeared that the continued diminution of Delos at the hands of the Athenians roused the wrath of Apollo; he was taken to be the source of the recurrence of plague in Athens in the winter of 426-425 B.C. Pericles had died in the preceding epidemic of 430–429. Since old prophecies stressed Apollo's hatred of death, a placatory purification of the entire island, similar to a previous purification of the area near the temple under Peisistratos, was undertaken: all tombs within sight of Apollo's shrine were removed to a common grave in Rheneia. Further, it was decreed that henceforth neither birth nor death should take place on Delos; women in labor and the dying were likewise conveyed across the channel.

But four years later, the Athenians again resumed pressure; they expelled all living inhabitants of the island to Asia Minor. This time Apollo's oracle at Delphi intervened, and survivors were allowed to return.

More and more, however, new settlers from Athens made the island into a colony; as such, until the eclipse of its patron city, it enjoyed great magnificence.

For a new festival, at five-yearly intervals, a sacred ship brought official Athenian representatives; the celebration was taken so seriously that while the delegation was away on this voyage, no death sentence was carried out in Athens. In the fourth of Plato's Socratic dialogues, Phaedo explains how such an absence deferred the execution after the trial of Socrates.

"It is the ship in which, according to Athenian tradition, Theseus went to Crete when he took with him the fourteen youths, and was the saviour of them and of himself. And they are said to have vowed to Apollo at the time, that if they were saved they would send a yearly mission to Delos. Now this custom still continues, and the whole period of the voyage to and from Delos, beginning when the priest of

Apollo crowns the stern of the ship, is a holy season, during which the city is not allowed to be polluted by public executions; and when the vessel is detained by contrary winds, the time spent in going and returning is very considerable. As I was saying, the ship was crowned on the day before the trial, and this was the reason why Socrates lay in prison and was not put to death until long after he was condemned."

The arrival at Delos of the delegation of 417 B.C. is described in Plutarch's *Life of Nicias*, who succeeded Pericles as leader of Athens and was the city's ranking representative on this occasion:

"His performances at Delos are, also, on record, as noble and magnificent works of devotion. For whereas the choruses which the cities sent to sing hymns to the god were wont to arrive in no order, as it might happen, and, being there met by a crowd of people crying out to them to sing, in their hurry to begin, used to disembark confusedly, putting on their garlands, and changing their dresses as they left the ships, he, when he had to convey the sacred company, disembarked the chorus at Rhenea, together with the sacrifice, and other holy appurtenances. And having brought along with him from Athens a bridge fitted by measurement for the purpose, and magnificently adorned with gilding and coloring, and with garlands and tapestries: this he laid in the night over the channel betwixt Rhenea and Delos, being no great distance. And at break of day he marched forth with all the procession to the god, and led the chorus, sumptuously ornamented, and singing their hymns, along over the bridge. The sacrifices, the games, and the feast being over, he set up a palm-tree of brass for a present to the god, and bought a parcel of land with ten thousand drachmas which he consecrated; with the revenue the inhabitants of Delos were to sacrifice and to feast, and to pray the gods for many good things to Nicias. This he engraved on a pillar, which he left in Delos to be a record of his bequest."

Enlivened in imagination with color, crowds, and sound of voices bargaining, disputing, chanting, the ruins of Delos become intelligible. The congestion of buildings at the water's edge of the sacred and the commercial port, even greater than that of Lower Manhattan, makes graphic the position of Delos as an entrepôt of seafarers, a city that lived from the sea.

There are prehistoric remains on the island—the Minoan fountain may trace back to Crete—but most of the more conspicuous early buildings were constructed in the seventh and sixth centuries by the Naxians. It was they who built the colossal statue of Apollo of which today only two pieces of the torso remain, abandoned part way to the sea by marauders who found them too great a burden. The statue originally stood on a base that can still be identified; it was first damaged when, in a storm, the bronze palm tree given by Nicias fell and toppled it over.

Most spectacular of the monuments that endure are the lions that flank a terrace at the farther end of the built-up area between the sea and the sacred lake, now dry, in whose center French archaeologists have planted a palm, the island's only tree, in memory of Leto. The lions are carved in archaic style, of Naxian marble; lithe and lean, sitting up instead of lying on their pedestals, they look far fitter for the chase than the zoo-fat guardians of London's Trafalgar Square.

Many of the city's largest buildings—cistern, waterworks, theater on the hill, and shrines, agoras, trading establishments, workrooms, shops near the water, were built fairly late, in the third and second centuries, for Delos had two further periods of prosperity under foreign dominion after the decay of Greece.

During the Macedonian empire, in the time of its dissolution and division among generals after the death of Alexander the Great, the Eastern Aegean was only nominally part of the Egyptian kingdom. The central islands formed a new union with independent Delos as its religious center, and much new building took place.

Following the conquest of Macedonia, the Romans again attached the island to Athens; to counterbalance the trading position of Rhodes, they made Delos a free port. After they wiped Corinth off the map in 146 B.C., Delos also took over much of that city's western Mediterranean transit commerce.

During this era, the island numbered residents from around the known world. Cults of many peoples—Serapis and Isis from Egypt, Atargatis from Syria, the Cabiri from Samothrace, Baal from Beirut— set up their altars. Guildsmen of all occupations—bankers, tradesmen, shipowners, even freedmen and slaves—built extensive edifices. Up the near slope of Mount Cynthos, Roman villas multiplied. Public baths were installed in one of the agoras; there was a hotel for visitors at ceremonial times; and on the other side of the island, a stadium for horse racing in addition to the ancient Delian games.

Well-preserved mosaics floor the Roman villas, showing designs with geometric perspective, theatrical masks, dolphins ridden by cupids, Dionysus riding a panther whose baleful snarl is complete even to twitching whiskers. In one house, stand statues of an Athenian Cleopatra and her husband Dioscourides.

The entire city can be well seen from the theater; the top of Mount Cynthos, 368 feet up, offers a panorama of the Cyclades.

Statues, vases, and other artifacts are in the museum, but the funeral steles that were once on Delos and then moved to Rheneia at the time of the purification are now in the museum of nearby Mykonos.

. Ranged in long rows, these steles are infinitely moving. Individually, some of the more imposing monuments from the Kerameikos at Athens and other burial places, now in the Archaeological Museum at Athens, may be more beautiful; they are certainly more elaborate. Many of

them, however, carry into death a social ostentation comparable to the competitive building of towers in Renaissance Italy; in both cases, such display eventually reached a point where it was halted by government order.

But on the steles of Delos, the memorial figures of the reliefs are relatively small; as one looks along the wall against which they stand, what is most evident is the pathos of their repeated gesture of farewell. The dead person, usually seated, is on one side, the living next-of-kin on the other; between them is the down-drooping U-curve of a relaxing handclasp, infinitely dignified and infinitely sad.

Then in 88 B.C., in one brutal carnage, the island of Delos became a collective funeral stele. The fleet of Mithridates descended in a surprise attack to punish the adherence of Delos to the arms of Rome.

Delos: Center of Trade

The slaughter may have annihilated as many as twenty thousand human beings; the city was systematically destroyed. An effort at recovery was crippled in 69 B.C. by a second piratical visitation: Pausanias describes the city's end:

> "In the days when Delos was a part of Greece, and traders were believed safe there under the protection of the god, Menophanes, general of Mithridates, knowing that the island was unfortified and the people unarmed, sailed to it with a fleet, massacred the population, foreigners and natives alike, looted much of the merchandise and all the votive offerings, sold the women and children into slavery, and razed the town of Delos to the ground. Whether he did it out of pure wantonness or by the express orders of Mithridates, who can tell? A covetous man thinks more of gain than of godliness."

Its people scattered, its buildings destroyed, its statues overturned, its forests of columns turned into a cutover area, Delos became again *adelos*, invisible.

CHAPTER 7 *Delphi: Political Prophecy*

AT Delphi as at Delos, the ranking god was
Apollo. But while at Delos he was the protector of a particular island,
at Delphi his oracle spoke to the whole Greek world. Only to Delphi
and to Olympia did citizens of all of the city-states come with equal
right. With occasional interruptions, the institutions of these two places
were shared over a territory as wide as that in which Hellenic customs
and speech were known. The Greek world found political unity only
fitfully and rarely, but it was consistently conscious of cultural unity,
and Delphi was a center to which all participants freely came.

At this shrine, the city-states met on what, if not common, was at
any rate neutral ground—and the inter-city subscriptions to restore
damage done to the shrine by periodic earthquakes and landslides
indeed almost made it common ground.

Delphi: Political Prophecy

Here, a geologic awe is ever-present. The 8,000-foot massif of Mount Parnassus is compounded of vast portents: snow-covered until late spring; darkly lowering thereafter; climbable—and then with caution—only during July and August; topped by wispy mists from whose shapes countrymen foretell the weather; often reverberating with immense thunder that seems indeed the very voice of the god. The area of the shrine, surrounded on three sides by steep upward slopes, and with a vertiginous gorge dropping to the river Pleistos as its fourth dimension, provides that voice with a colossal amphitheater.

The original shrine on this site was that of a dragon named Python. But wayfaring men coming from the Gulf of Corinth through the Gulf of Itea found access here to the land passages across central and into northern Greece, and among these far voyagers were men from Crete who introduced the worship of Apollo Delphinios—Apollo of the Dolphin; he prevailed over the Python, and as Pythian Apollo henceforth ruled the shrine.

Similarly, when the invading Dorians brought with them the worship of Herakles, Apollo struggled with him as he had with the dragon for possession of the prophetic tripod, and again prevailed.

But like Olympia and unlike most Greek institutions, the shrine at Delphi did not become an exclusive perquisite of a single city-state. An Amphictyonic League, representing twelve Greek peoples, was established to administer the shrine and manage the Pythian Games, held in honor of Apollo, first at eight-year intervals and quadrennially after 590 B.C. The festivals began with sacrifices and dramatic presentations of the victory of the god over the snake, followed by musical and choral contests, and then by athletic games in the stadium above the sanctuary and chariot races down in the valley hippodrome; victors were crowned with the sacred laurel.

Consultation of the oracle followed a fixed procedure. In preparation for voicing the words of the god, his priestess—in casting the part,

121

middle-aged peasant women were preferred—bathed in the Kastalian fountain, drank from the spring called Kassotis, inhaled vapors of laurel and barley, chewed leaves of laurel. Then, seated on a tripod in the underground adytum of the temple, she prophesied.

At the temple, two priests with life tenure were assisted by functionaries who arranged for consultations, prophets who turned the words of the babbling prophetess into rhyme, exegetics who interpreted the rhymes, and sacred slaves.

Pilgrims desiring a consultation—the privilege was confined to men—offered sacrifices; if, on examination, these were found acceptable, the inquirer was admitted to put his question to the Pythia.

At the museum in Jannina shards inscribed with questions asked of Zeus' oracle at Dodona indicate that many of the queries presented were the pathetic personalia that down the centuries have been the soothsayer's stock in trade: shall I take a journey; is my business venture sound; is the child my wife is carrying really mine? But interspersed among these private matters, often enough to affect Greek history, were portentous questions of state.

Descriptions of the life of Greek city-states normally emphasize the absence of theocratic dominance: in their politics, neither officially nor in fact was the priesthood a power. Propitiatory and votive offerings, sacrifices, and festivals were part of public panoply, but public policy was made in the agora, and by the citizenry, not in the temple by the priesthood. And because the Greek city-states were connected only by loose and shifting leagues, there was no question of ecclesiastical influence on a central government.

Yet the oracle at Delphi was a frequent source of political initiative. City-states, from Asia Minor to Magna Graecia, consulted the Delphic oracle on many of their major moves. Even kings of other territories, like Croesus and Gyges of Lydia in the sixth century B.C., and Philip of Macedonia in the fourth, sent offerings. The shrine at its height was

an unequaled center of political intelligence; confusing, and subject to double interpretation as its counsel might be, the oracle was an initiating force in public affairs which repeatedly changed the course of history.

The decision made by the Athenians in 480 B.C., after consultation first with the oracle and then among themselves, to abandon Athens and meet the Persians at sea at Salamis, is the most telling illustration of the effect of the oracle as a temporal power.

Herodotus, in his *History*, gives what until two years ago was the most reliable available version of what happened:

"When the Athenians, anxious to consult the oracle, sent their messengers to Delphi, hardly had the envoys completed the customary rites about the sacred precinct, and taken their seats inside the sanctuary of the god, when the priestess, Aristonice by name, thus prophesied:

> *Wretches, why sit ye here? Fly, fly to the ends of creation,*
> *Quitting your homes, and the crags which your city*
> *crowns with her circlet.*
> *Neither the head, nor the body is firm in its place,*
> *nor at bottom*
> *Firm the feet, nor the hands, nor resteth the middle*
> *uninjur'd.*
> *All—all ruined and lost. Since fire, and impetuous*
> *Ares,*
> *Speeding along in a Syrian chariot, hastes to destroy*
> *her.*
> *Not alone shalt thou suffer; full many the towers he*
> *will level,*
> *Many the shrines of the gods he will give to fiery*
> *destruction.*
> *Even now they stand with dark sweat horribly dripping,*

Delphi: Political Prophecy

> Trembling and quaking for fear, and lo! from the high
>   roofs trickleth
> Black blood, sign prophetic of hard distresses impending.
> Get ye away from the temple, and brood on the ills that
>   await ye!

"When the Athenian messengers heard this reply, they were filled with the deepest affliction; whereupon Timon, son of Androbulus, one of the men of most mark among the Delphians, seeing how utterly cast down they were at the gloomy prophecy, advised them to take an olive-branch, and entering the sanctuary again, consult the oracle as suppliants. The Athenians followed this advice, and going in once more, said, "O king! we pray thee reverence these boughs of supplication which we bear in our hands, and deliver to us something more comforting concerning our country. Else we will not leave thy sanctuary, but will stay here till we die." Upon this the priestess gave them a second answer, which was the following:

> Pallas has not been able to soften the lord of Olympus,
> Though she has often prayed him, and urged him with
>   excellent counsel.
> Yet once more I address thee in words than adamant
>   firmer.
> When the foe shall have taken whatever the limit of
>   Cecrops
> Holds within it, and all which divine Cithaeron shelters,
> Then far-seeing Zeus grants this to the prayers of
>   Athena;
> Safe shall the wooden wall continue for thee and thy
>   children.
> Wait not till the tramp of the horse, nor the footmen
>   mightily moving
> Over the land, but turn your back to the foe, and retire ye.

Yet shall a day arrive when ye shall meet him in battle.
Holy Salamis, thou shalt destroy the offspring of women
When men scatter the seed, or when they gather the
      harvest.

"This answer seemed, as indeed it was, gentler than the former one; so the envoys wrote it down, and went back with it to Athens. When, however, upon their arrival, they produced it before the people, and inquiry began to be made into its true meaning; many and various were the interpretations which men put upon it; two, more especially, seemed to be directly opposed to one another. Certain of the old men were of opinion that the god meant to tell them the citadel would escape; for this was anciently defended by a palisade; and they supposed that barrier to be the wooden wall of the oracle. Others maintained that the fleet was what the god pointed at; and their advice was that nothing should be thought of except the ships, which had best be at once got ready. Still such as said the wooden wall meant the fleet, were perplexed by the last two lines of the oracle—

Holy Salamis, thou shalt destroy the offspring of women
When men scatter the seed, or when they gather the
      harvest.

These words caused great disturbance among those who took the wooden wall to be the ships; since the interpreters understood them to mean, that, if they made preparations for a sea-fight, they would suffer a defeat off Salamis.

"Now there was at Athens a man who had lately made his way into the first rank of citizens; his true name was Themistocles; but he was known more generally as the son of Neocles. This man came forward and said, that the interpreters had not explained the oracle altogether aright, "For if," he argued, "the clause in question had really respected the Athenians, it would not have been expressed so mildly; the phrase used would have been 'Luckless Salamis' rather than 'Holy Salamis,' had those to whom the island belonged been about to perish in its neighborhood. Rightly taken, the response of the god threatened the enemy, much more than the Athenians." He therefore counseled his countrymen to make ready to fight on board their ships, since they were the wooden wall in which the god told them to trust. When Themistocles had thus cleared the matter, the Athenians embraced his view, preferring it to that of the interpreters."

Herodotus' account, however, was written some thirty to forty years after the event; a partial revision of his story, indicating that the evacuation of Athens, rather than a last-minute effort to "fly to the ends of creation," was part of an orderly strategic plan, is offered by a source that suddenly became available in 1959.

It was found when an American professor on an overseas fellowship inquired of villagers in the town of Troezen in the northern Peloponnese whether there were any ancient inscriptions in the locality. He was taken to a nearby coffeehouse, which exhibited a stone some two feet tall and one foot broad. On it was inscribed the plan offered by Themistocles and adopted by the Athenians in public assembly some two months before the battle of Thermopylae, outlining exactly what everyone was to do.

This record of the details of the decision on which the future of the Greeks as a free people in all likelihood depended not only ranks with the great documents of liberty in the West, from Magna Carta to the Declaration of Independence; it was their essential precursor. For the extinction of free inquiry in the Greek cities of Asia Minor after they were conquered in the previous century is compelling evidence of what would have happened in Greece proper under the same domination. The reason that the inscription was at Troezen—it is now in Athens—is implied in its text: in 480, the town became the evacuation center for the Athenian women and children. It was natural that this should be so, for legend cited Troezen as the home of the hero Pittheus, and it was his daughter, pregnant by King Aegeus of Athens, who bore Theseus, that king's future heir.

With parentheses indicating uncertainties due to damage to the stone, the tablet reads:

The Gods.
Resolved by the Councils and the People on the motion of Themisto-
kles, son of Neokles, of the deme Phrearrhoi: to entrust the city to
Athena the Mistress of Athens and to all the other gods to guard and
defend from the Barbarian the sake of the land. The Athenians them-
selves and the foreigners who live in Athens are to evacuate their chil-
dren and women to Troezen . . . the ARCHEGETES of the land. . . .
The old men and the moveable possessions are to be removed to Sa-
lamis. The treasurers and the priestesses are to remain on the acropolis
protecting the possessions of the gods.

All the other Athenians and foreigners of military age are to embark
on the 200 ships that lie ready and defend against the Barbarian for the
sake of their own freedom and that of the rest of the Greeks, along with
the Lakedaimonians, the Corinthians, the Aiginetans and all others who
wish to share the danger.

The generals are to appoint, starting tomorrow, 200 trierarchs, one
to a ship, from among those who have ancestral land in Athens and
legitimate children and who are not older than fifty; to these men the
ships are to be assigned by lot. They are also to enlist marines, 20 to a
ship, from men between the age of twenty and thirty, and four archers
to a ship. They are also to assign the petty officers to the ships at the
same time that they allot the trierarchs. The generals are also to write
up the names of the crews of the ships on white boards, taking the
names of the Athenians from the lexiarchic registers, the foreigners from

those registered with the polemarch. They are to write up the names assigning the whole number to 200 equal divisions, and to write above each division the name of the trireme and the trierarch and the petty officers so that each division may know on which trireme it is to embark. When all the divisions have been composed and allotted to the triremes, the Council and the generals are to complete the manning of the 200 ships, after sacrificing a placatory offering to Zeus the Almighty, Athena, Victory, and Poseidon the Securer.

When the manning of the ships has been completed, with one hun-
dred of them they are to meet the enemy at Artemision in Euboia, and
with the other hundred of them they are to lie off Salamis and the rest
of Attika and keep guard over the land.

In order that all Athenians may be united in their defense against the
Barbarian, those who have been sent into exile for ten years are to go
to Salamis and to stay there until the People come to some decision
about them, while those who have been deprived of citizen rights. . . .

On-the-spot evidence of Delphi's political importance is written large
both in the treasuries of the various city-states there, and in the national
monuments which line the Sacred Way to the shrine. Patriotism peopled this neutral area with allegorical groups and statues of heroes; it
was unembarrassed by the fact that many of the deeds celebrated had
been at the expense of other city-states whose monuments might
occupy adjacent locations.

For instance, across the way from the Athenian monument that com-
memorated the exploits of Miltiades at Marathon is the ex voto of the
Athenians' ranking enemy, the Spartans; in front of it is a monument
by which the Arcadians recalled their part in the defeat of the Spartans
—actually accomplished chiefly by the Thebans—at the battle of Leuctra
in 371 B.C.

There were so many of these monuments that their enumeration fills
twenty-seven close-packed pages of Pausanias' patient census; and he
saw them after much pillage, including Nero's removal of some five
hundred during a single imperial progress.

Among city-state treasuries, that of Athens has been reassembled; it
is at the turn beyond which the Sacred Way passes the earliest area to be
venerated on Parnassus, the rough rocks that marked the first seat of
the Sybil, where the drama of Apollo's killing of the Python was quadrennially re-enacted as part of the celebration of the Pythian games.

Delphi: Political Prophecy

Like its counterpart at Olympia, this primitive sanctuary, lying dark and disordered in the midst of form and symmetry, hinting at hidden horrors of a blind and animate earth, dumbly evidencing the power of the elements to crush emerging man, provides the base line of a scale from which to measure the levels reached by Greek civilization and Greek art.

Erected after 548 B.C., behind and to the south of this shrine lies the polygonal wall whose stones surface the terrace on which the temple of Apollo stands. Much later, it came to serve a second purpose as an archives center. Over seven hundred inscriptions, carved on its face, date and document various events; most of them are records of the freeing of slaves.

The ex votos along the last lap as the Sacred Way reaches the shrine emphasize the range of territory over which the oracle was venerated: here in the Treasury of Corinth were kept the offerings of the Lydian kings; there stood a golden chariot dedicated to the Sun God by the citizens of another of his territories, Rhodes; yonder were tripods from the Syracusan tyrants, Gelo and Hiero, celebrating their victories over the Carthaginians.

Mists often silhouette the three re-erected upright colums of massive stuccoed tufa at the ruin of Apollo's temple. It was built in Doric style in the middle of the fourth century B.C., after a major earthquake had destroyed its predecessor. The walls of the entrance portal were inscribed with sayings of sages: "Know thyself"; "Everything in moderation." On the ground level were statues of Poseidon, of Apollo, of the Fates. The secular treasures of the interior included a statue of Homer and the iron chair in which Pindar sat when he came to Delphi to sing odes to Apollo; in an epitaph, Antipater of Sidon said of him and them:

> This earth holds Pindar, the Pierian trumpet, the heavily smiting smith of well-outlined hymns, whose melody when thou hearest thou

131

*wouldst exclaim that a swarm of bees from the muses fashioned it in
the bridal chamber of Cadmus.*

Below ground level were the central chambers of the shrine, the
waiting room and the adytum. The adytum contained the omphalos,
a stone which was regarded as the navel of the world; a gilded Apollo;
the tomb of Dionysus; and the tripod on which the Pythia sat to inhale
trance-producing fumes.

Around the shrine, both down the mountain from it and higher up
the slope, are the buildings erected for the Pythian festival.

At some distance to the east, lower than the Kastalian spring, are the
.gymnasium, complete with running track, where the athletes trained,
and the palaestra, containing baths, where wrestlers were rubbed with
oil before their contests.

These are above the point where the road from Athens reaches the
sacred area, marked by the shrine of Athena Pronaia, Athena-guardian-
of-the-temple. Among its buildings is a tholos comparable to that at the
shrine of Asklepios at Epidauros; three columns and their entablature
have been re-erected.

The theater where some five thousand people could watch the dramatic and choral contests of the festival is up the mountain from the
temple. In earlier years, the seating consisted of earth terraces cut into
the slope like those at Olympia; a benefaction of Herodes Atticus
provided the present stone facings both here and in the stadium.

East of the theater grew a grove of the sacred laurel; beyond it was a
large building, dedicated by the Knidians about 450 B.C. as a clubroom,
or place to talk. The interior of this building, even as late as Pausanias'
time, was decorated with two tremendous frescoes, one showing the departure of the Greeks from Troy after the fall of Ilion, the other based
on Homer's description of the visit of Odysseus to the kingdom of the
dead. The artist was the Thasian Polygnotus. With minute detail on

color and pose, Pausanias describes the multitude of identifiable personages in these paintings, their expression, their dress, their rings, their lyres, their garlands, their dice, their pitchers. His pages reemphasize the tragedy of the close-to-total disappearance of one of the major classic arts.

Delphi: Political Prophecy

A further steep climb leads to the stadium, where some six thousand spectators could see the athletic contests. The marble start-and-finish lines are still there, with grooves for the placing of runners' feet at take-off, and holes for the insertion of staves to separate runner from runner.

The hippodrome was in the valley, on the plain where the breath-taking gorge of the Pleistos widens to approach the Itean Gulf, and where now, coral-like, the contiguous branches of tens of thousands of venerable olive trees form a gray-green inland sea. This is the view down and across which the traveler looks from the hotels of the new Delphi—when the French School began its excavations, its first agenda was to move the town of Krissa, then planted squarely atop the ruins, to its present location slightly farther northwest.

Post-war reconstruction is nearly complete at the museum above the road which leads from the shrine to the new town; after orienting themselves at the ruins, visitors can readorn the shrine in imagination with the statues, the friezes, the metopes that are here protected.

Among the pieces that were parts of buildings is the frieze from the Siphnian Treasury showing a battle between gods and giants, and that of the Athenian Treasury which displays a battle of Greeks with Amazons and the struggle in which Herakles overcame the lion of Nemea. Pre-eminent among statues is the bronze Charioteer, the lithe youth in a long draped chiton whose controlled face belies the tension in the muscles of his hands and feet. Who was he? No one knows, though his statue is thought to date between 480–470 B.C. and it was dedicated by Polyzalos of Gela in Sicily. But he is very like the young Karrhotos, celebrated in Pindar's fourth and fifth Pythian odes, who in 462 B.C. won the chariot race for his brother-in-law, Arkesilas, king of the Greek colony in today's Libya. Because, as in contemporary horse racing, the prize in a chariot race was awarded to the owner rather than the jockey,

135

Pindar's odes are dedicated to Arkesilas, but Karrhotos is duly celebrated therein. Here is how Pindar praised both victors:

Wide is the strength of wealth
when mixed with stainless virtue
and, granted of destiny, mortal man leads it home,
most dear companion.
Arkesilas, God's destiny is on you;
from the towering stairs
of your renowned life
you approach it in glory
by Kastor's favor, of the golden chariot,
who, after storm of winter, makes
your hearth shine in the blessed quiet.

Even power granted of God
is carried the better for wisdom.
You walk in righteousness, and great prosperity is unceasing
about you,
twice over: since you are king
of great cities,
for this high privilege
is a shining heritage in your house,
which matches your own temper;
and blessed are you even now, in that,
winning from the famed Pythiad success with horses, your
prayer's end,
you are given this festal choir of men,

delight of Apollo; whereby, forget not,
as you are sung at Kyrene's sweet garden of Aphrodite,
to ascribe all cause to God
and love Karrhotos beyond all companions.

136

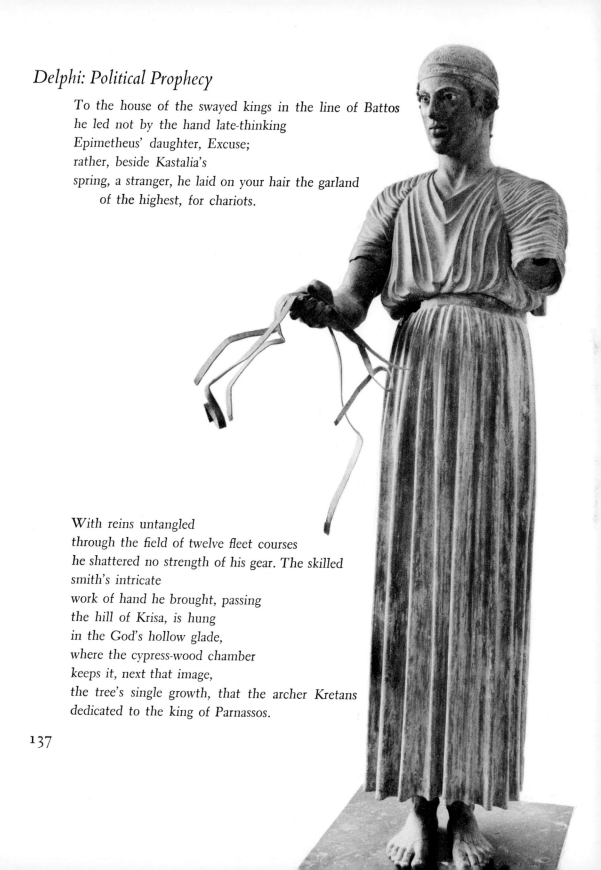

Delphi: Political Prophecy

To the house of the swayed kings in the line of Battos
he led not by the hand late-thinking
Epimetheus' daughter, Excuse;
rather, beside Kastalia's
spring, a stranger, he laid on your hair the garland
    of the highest, for chariots.

With reins untangled
through the field of twelve fleet courses
he shattered no strength of his gear. The skilled
smith's intricate
work of hand he brought, passing
the hill of Krisa, is hung
in the God's hollow glade,
where the cypress-wood chamber
keeps it, next that image,
the tree's single growth, that the archer Kretans
dedicated to the king of Parnassos.

With fain heart it becomes you
now to greet him. He has done well.
Son of Alexibias, the fair-haired Graces flare about you.
Blessed are you, that even
after the huge toil
you have remembrance in mighty
words. Among forty
charioteers who fell, you brought
perfect your car through, and with heart unshaken,
and are come home from the shining of the games'
prizes to the plain of Libya and the city of your fathers. . . .

CHAPTER 8 *Olympia: The Greek Games*

O LYMPIA, the site of the Panhellenic Games, lies a little to the west of Arcadia, the mountain-girt fastness in the northern Peloponnese around which the tides of migration and war washed harmlessly through the centuries, but it lies close enough to partake of its deep tranquillity. Here, in a pastoral setting at the confluence of the rivers Alpheios and Kladeos, the air is often so still that bees sound strident; the hovering of a hummingbird-moth is audible.

No sharper contrast could be found than that between the sites of Delphi and Olympia; yet in the one as in the other the word "Hellas"— "all of Greece"—had a substantial meaning.

Every four years, heralds—*spondophoroi*—made the rounds of the Hellenic world to announce the exact dates on which the next Olympic

139

Games would be held, and to declare a sacred truce covering both the selected week of full moon between July and September and the time used for training and in travel by participants and spectators; the truce was effective from the Western Mediterranean to Asia Minor.

During the truce, athletes and spectators came from the wind's four quarters without hindrance on sea or land, and returned recounting names of heroes who would thenceforth be honored not only in their native cities but by Greeks everywhere.

Just when the games were first instituted is a matter of legend; but precise dates define more than a millennium of these quadrennial festivals—the Greeks called them quinquennial because they counted the year that was the end of one period and the beginning of another as two years. The first games precisely known to be celebrated were held in 776 B.C.; they were discontinued in A.D. 393. Greek history was reckoned from Olympiad to Olympiad.

Triumphs at Olympia were personal triumphs. In Delphi, most of the myriad statues celebrated exploits which had enhanced the power or secured the survival of city-states; in Olympia, most of them celebrated the prowess of an individual.

Diversity of legend gives conflicting antecedents for the games.

According to one version, Herakles founded the games, and Olympian Zeus, his father, became their patron. In turn, the hill above Olympia was named Mount Kronion in honor of Zeus' father.

An alternative legend cites the mythological hero Pelops as the inaugurator; his story is recounted by the statuary of the entrance pediment of the Temple of Zeus. Pelops was said to have come as a young prince from Asia Minor to contest the hand of the horse-taming maiden, Hippodameia, daughter of Oinomaos, the Arcadian king who also ruled over Pisa, the state that contained Olympia, and Elis, the next state to the west. The father's custom was to challenge suitors to a chariot race, with Hippodameia the prize but death the lot of the unsuccessful.

Olympia: The Greek Games

Until Pelops' arrival, the wind-begotten mares of Oinomaos, Psylla and Harpinna, had outdistanced all comers. But Pelops bribed Myrtilos, the king's charioteer, to replace with wax the linchpins of the paternal chariot wheels; Oinomaos plunged to his death and Pelops lived to marry the daughter, start the games, and give his name to the Peloponnese.

In his third Olympian ode Pindar tells how it was likewise Pelops who brought the wild olive to Olympia:

> . . . But the lawn in the valley of Kronian Pelops had blossomed
>   not to the beauty of trees.
> He thought the garden, naked of these, must endure the
>   sun's sharp rays.
> There it was the urge took him to journey
>
> to Istrian country. There Leto's daughter, the runner with
>   horses,
> received him when he came from Arkadia's ridges and
>   winding gullies,
> when, at Eurystheus' command,
> the doom of his father had driven him
> to bring the doe with the golden horns
> that once Taygeta had written in fee
> to be sacred to Artemis Orthosia.
>
> On that errand he saw the land at the back of the cold north
>   wind,
> and he stood amazed at the trees.
> A sweet longing came upon him to plant them at the twelve-
>   lap running place
> of horses. . . .

Olympia: The Greek Games

The games began as an incidental part of a religious festival, but over the centuries the religious aspect lessened, the athletic grew. The buildings at Olympia express both purposes.

In the center is the Altis, the sacred area, a formerly walled quadrilateral said to have been delineated by Herakles. This sacred precinct, still further back in the dark past, saw primitive worship of the earth-goddess Gaia; a deeply excavated altar, fetishly formless, recalls the lair of the python at Delphi.

From early times, the Altis contained an open altar to Zeus; and Pelops had a shrine on a small rise. The level of Zeus' altar was annually raised: the priests made cement by mixing the ashes of the bones of the animals sacrificed on it with the waters of the river Alpheios. By Pausanias' time, the height had reached twenty-two feet.

The earliest actual temple, going back to perhaps 1000 B.C., was that of Hera. The present ruins are of a seventh century Doric building thought to be the third on the site; it is the oldest extant temple in Greece. A colossal head of the goddess, probably from the temple's central statue, was also found by excavators.

But the glory of the sacred area was the temple of Zeus, built between 468 and 456 B.C. and therefore contemporary with the great temple built by Greek colonists at Paestum in Italy, and slightly senior to the Parthenon. Just as the acquisition of the Delian treasure made the building in Athens possible, so the spoils taken by the west-coast men of Elis when they won a war with the Pisans for control of the Olympian area swelled this building fund.

The structure is colossal; the upper level of the stylobate is 200 feet long and just over 90 wide; Pausanias said that the height from the base of the pillars, of which there were thirteen on the sides and six at the ends, to the apex of the marble-tiled wooden roof was slightly more than 66 feet. The columns were just over 34 feet in height, comparable to but more massive than those of the Parthenon; they were of stone,

143

coated with painted stucco. Some of them now lie with their component sections in complete order, as they fell when toppled by an earthquake in the sixth century A.D.

The chryselephantine statue of Zeus, some forty feet high, within this sanctuary was the work of Pheidias; the workshop where he and his collaborators wrought for years has been identified, including a shard inscribed, "Pheidias, his cup." The statue, studded with glass and possibly with semiprecious stones, was regarded as one of the Seven Wonders of the World; it stood in place until carried off to Constantinople under the Emperor Theodosius II; it was destroyed in a fire there in A.D. 475.

Pausanias set down a meticulous description of it, which gives a glimpse of the color and the splendor of the sacred precinct as it was through successive periods in the great days of the Games:

"The god is seated in a throne: he is made of gold and ivory: on his head is a wreath made in imitation of sprays of olive. In his right hand he carries a Victory, also of ivory and gold: she wears a ribbon, and on her head a wreath. In the left hand of the god is a sceptre, curiously wrought in all the metals: the bird perched on the sceptre is the eagle. The sandals of the god are of gold, and so is his robe. On the robe are wrought figures of animals and the lily flowers.

"The throne is adorned with gold and precious stones, also with ebony and ivory; and there are figures painted and images wrought on it. There are four Victories, in the attitude of dancing, at each foot of the throne, and two others are at the bottom of each foot. On each of the two front feet are Theban children carried off by sphinxes, and under the sphinxes Apollo and Artemis are shooting down the children of Niobe with arrows. Between the feet of the throne are four bars, each extending from foot to foot. On the bar which faces the entrance there are seven images: the eighth image has disappeared, they know not how. These may be representations of the ancient contests, for the contests for boys were not yet instituted at the time of Phidias. They say that the boy binding his head with a ribbon is a likeness of Pantarces, an Elean youth, said to have been a favorite of Phidias. Pantarces won a victory in the boys' wrestling match in the eighty-sixth Olympiad. On the other bars is the troop that fought on the side of Hercules against the Amazons. The total number of figures is twenty-nine. Theseus is arrayed amongst the allies of Hercules.

"The throne is supported not by the feet only, but by an equal number of pillars which stand between the feet. But it is not possible to go under the throne in the way that we pass into the interior of the throne at Amyclae; for in Olympia people are kept off by barriers made like walls. Of these barriers, the one facing the door is painted blue simply: the rest exhibit paintings by Panaenus. Amongst these paintings is seen Atlas upholding heaven and earth, and beside him stands Hercules wishing to take the burden of Atlas on himself; also Theseus and Pirithous, and Greece and Salamis holding in her hand the figure-head of a ship; and there is the struggle of Hercules with the Nemean lion; and the outrage offered by Ajax to Cassandra; and Hippodamia, daughter of Oenomaus, with her mother; and Prometheus still in fetters, and Hercules is borne up aloft to him; for one of the stories about Hercules is that he killed the eagle that was torturing Prometheus on the Caucasus, and freed him from his fetters. The last paintings are Penthesilea giving up the ghost and Achilles supporting her, and two Hesperids bearing the apples, with the keeping of which they are said to have been entrusted. This Panaenus was a brother of Phidias, and the painting of the battle of Marathon in the Painted Colonnade at Athens is by him. On the uppermost parts of the throne, above the head of the image, Phidias has made, on one side, the Graces, and on the other side the Seasons, three of each; for in poetry the Seasons also are described as daughters of Zeus, and in the Iliad Homer says that the Seasons had charge of the sky, just like the guards of a king's court. The footstool, or as people in Attica like to call it, the thranion, under the feet of

Zeus has golden lions, and the battle of Theseus with the Amazons is wrought in relief on it. This battle was the first deed of valour done by the Athenians against foreign foes.

"On the pedestal, which supports the throne and the whole gorgeous image of Zeus, there are figures of gold, the Sun mounted in a car, and Zeus and Hera . . . and beside him one of the Graces, and next to her Hermes, and next to Hermes Hestia; and after Hestia there is Love receiving Aphrodite as she rises from the sea, and Persuasion is crowning Aphrodite. Apollo, too, and Artemis are wrought in relief on it, and Athena and Hercules; and at the end of the pedestal Amphitrite and

Poseidon, and the Moon riding what seems to me a horse. Some say, however, that the goddess is riding a mule, and not a horse, and they tell a silly story about the mule.

"I know that the measurements of the height and breadth of Zeus at Olympia have been recorded, but I cannot commend the men who took the measurements. For even the measurements they mention fall far short of the impression made by the image on the spectator. Why, the god himself, they say, bore witness to the art of Phidias. For when the image was completed Phidias prayed that the god would give a sign if the work was to his mind, and straightway, they say, the god hurled a thunderbolt into the ground at the spot where the bronze urn stood down to my time.

"The ground in front of the image is flagged, not with white, but with black stone. Round about the black pavement runs a raised edge of Parian marble to keep in the olive oil which is poured out. For oil

is good for the image at Olympia, and it is this that keeps the ivory from suffering through the marshy situation of the Altis. But on the Acropolis at Athens it is not oil, but water, that is good for the ivory image of the Virgin. For the Acropolis being dry, by reason of its great height, the ivory image needs water and moisture. At Epidaurus, when I asked why they poured neither water nor oil on the image of Aesculapius, the attendants of the sanctuary told me that the image and throne of the god were erected over a well."

This awesome and marvelous figure was thus the presiding presence in the Altis.

The staging of the religious festivals that culminated in this shrine, and the management of the games, from maintenance of buildings for the athletes to provision of judges and umpires and entertainment of visiting celebrities, was, after the defeat of the Pisans, under the jurisdiction of an Elean Council. The Council sat in the Bouleuterion, to the south of the temple of Zeus; this building contained the statue of Zeus Horkios—Zeus the protector of oaths—in front of which contestants in the games took an oath of sportsmanship on the initial day.

Northwest of the Heraion, in which Aristotle reported seeing a bronze disc inscribed with the laws of the festivals, was a further official building, the Prytaneion, a refectory for the priests and magistrates of the Altis, and the scene of official banquets during the games. In this building, too, was the public hearth of the Olympian Amphictyony, where an eternal flame burned to the goddess Hestia.

Along the eastern end of the north wall of the Altis, a series of treasuries, originally twelve in number, in the form of small temples, was erected by various city-states, particularly those of Sicily and South Italy.

To the west of the Altis were houses for the priests and a Heroön;

148

among heroes revered here were Iamos and Klytios, leaders of two ancient families of Olympian soothsayers.

These buildings were in existence in the fifth century B.C. They were eventually flanked by further buildings, some dating from Macedonian, some from Roman times, in which Hellenistic art and architecture provided a mixture of grandeur, ostentation, and creature comfort.

On the west, opposite the magistrates' hall, a gymnasium provided a practice ground for foot races sheltered from heat and rain; next to it was a palaestra where athletes could train for wrestling and boxing matches, cleanse themselves with sand, rub themselves with oil, and avail themselves of the conveniences which accompanied latter-day preoccupation with plumbing. Herodus Atticus provided an aqueduct that led water to a fountain on the slope beyond the Heraion to assuage the thirst of the general public.

Normally, aspirants for the contests trained for a time at Elis; the best were then admitted to competition at Olympia, and went there for final training.

Above the Kladeos, beyond the gymnasium and palaestra, were Roman baths, and a Roman house was built close to Pheidias' workshop; the southwest corner of the area surrounding the Altis was occupied by a very large edifice of the late fourth century B.C. dedicated to Zeus by Leonidas of Naxos and used for the accommodation of official visitors.

The southeast corner of the Altis was bounded by the house that lodged the Emperor Nero during his visit in A.D. 66–67; north of it was the long frescoed stoa known as the Portico of the Echo, perhaps built by Philip of Macedon.

At the northeast corner is the entrance, vaulted over in Roman times with a 100-foot tunnel, through which the athletes passed as they flocked to the stadium.

Olympia: The Greek Games

The contests which took them there developed in variety over time. Earliest of recorded games, at a time when the festival lasted but one day, were the foot races; throughout the Olympiads, winners of these outranked all others in prestige. The length of the stadium track is 192.27 meters; the limestone start-and-finish lines, with their slotted toe holds, are there today. Races included the "short" race, down a single course; a double course; a multiple course. In the latter part of the sixth century B.C. a race for men in full armor, the "hoplites race," was added.

The pentathlon, a combination of five events—jumping, javelin throwing, foot racing, discus throwing, and wrestling—was inaugurated in 708 B.C. At the beginning of the sixth century, the pankration, a combination of boxing and wrestling, was introduced.

Contests between men in the stadium were complemented in the mid-seventh century B.C., first by two- and four-horse chariot races, then by horse races; riders used neither stirrups nor saddle.

During the classical period, the week of the games began with the giving of the oath in which competitors swore to abide by the rules and not to "use tricks in order to force victory." Just to the left of the stadium entrance, a series of bronze statues to Zeus known as Zanes, built with the fines of oath-breaking contestants, afforded a last-minute warning.

At the conclusion of the contests, the final day was devoted to pomp and ceremony. The pageantry of the games, with the beautiful nude bodies of the contestants set off against the rich robes of the magistrates, visiting officials, and wealthy spectators then reached its climax.

Through the week, at the end of each event, the winner was given a palm frond. On the final day, the victors were crowned in the central sanctuary, before the colossal statue of Zeus, with wreaths cut from the sacred wild olive. A three-time winner had the right to have his statue erected in the Altis.

The religious overtones of the ceremony re-emphasized the value of the well-trained body and the well-trained mind that was central to the symmetry of Greek thought. Spectators at Olympia included philosophers and poets. The triumphant athlete was a subject for sculptors, painters, and bards; his return to his native city-state was an occasion for

public rejoicing and the conferring of communal favors; frequently, the image of a victorious chariot was reproduced on the city's coins.

Pindar's odes commemorate victors of all of the great mainland games: the laurel-crowned of the Pythian Games at Delphi; the wild celery-crowned of the Isthmian Games at Corinth; the pine-crowned of the Nemean Games at Nemea; as well as the olive-crowned at Olympia. In his fourteenth Olympian ode, to a fatherless lad who won the boys' short foot race in 476 B.C., he sang:

> . . . Go now, Echo, to the black wall
> of the house of Persephone, bring to his father the clear message;
> stand in the presence of Kleodamos and say that his son
> in the renowned valley of Pisa
> has put on his young hair the wings of glory for games won.

If the color of the peopled pageant must be re-created wholly through the imagination, the color of its templed background can be guessed from hints that still remain in the Olympian museum, for some of the finds unearthed in the nineteenth century bear traces of their original brilliant polychrome.

After the games were discontinued, the temples repeatedly pillaged, and the monuments shaken by earthquake, the desolate area was buried from three directions. Silt from Mount Kronion washed down; silt from the two adjacent rivers washed up. The Alpheios flooded out the hippodrome altogether, and one corner of the stadium. The Kladeos poured gravel around the central shrines. Eventually, a small Byzantine town sprangled over the site; parts of Pheidias' workshop were covered by a Byzantine church. Through the centuries, fallen monuments disappeared beneath a cumulative deposit which, when the German School began excavations, measured vertically some fifteen to twenty feet from surface to ancient ground level; current erosion of the stadium banks shows how quickly earth accumulates. Because of this burial, many artifacts remained which otherwise would surely have been ground up for lime, used for buildings elsewhere, or pillaged intact.

Among recovered statues, conjectural remountings in the museum show figures from the two pediments of the temple of Zeus, the story of Pelops from the east front, and from the West front the story of the disruption by drunken centaurs of the wedding ceremony of the Lapith prince Peirithoös and his bride Deidameia. Metopes from this temple display the labors of Herakles.

Two major individual statues were found with unbelievably little damage. Across from the entrance to the temple of Zeus, on a triangular base which is still in place, stood a statue of Victory offered by the Naupaktians and the Messenians toward the end of the fifth century. The goddess is caught at the moment when, descending from the sky, her foot is about to touch earth; she is the work of Paionios.

In the north room of the museum, alone, in perfect light and a monotone setting, stands the Parian marble statue of Hermes and the infant Dionysus found in the Heraion. The original of this statue was carved by Praxiteles; archaeologists disagree as to whether this is actually the original—and hence the only known example of work by this sculptor as it came from his hand—or whether it is a later copy. The god's upraised arm is partly missing: what was in the hand, to cause the baby to regard it so intensely? Evidence exists to suggest that it was a bunch of grapes, but as Hermes looks at the child, his attitude is that of one who not only looks but listens.

From a visit to Olympia, two impressions remain, differing in almost every quality.

One is of the sanctuary in its heyday. The surrounding hillsides are covered with tenting spectators from the whole Greek world, ready to crowd the forty-five thousand capacity of the stadium. Potentates are elaborately present from around the entire basin of the Mediterranean. Hawkers make the place a vast fair. Poets converse with philosophers.

Trainers of men and of horses tune contestants to concert pitch. Priest-led processions push and crowd the exits and the entrances of the Altis. Emotions range from the tenseness of expectation through the strain of performance to the pangs of defeat and the exaltation of success. There is noise and dust; colors are bright; bodies glisten.

The other impression is of the sanctuary now, muted in sound, even against footfall, by a carpet of pine needles from the grove which seeded itself at the time of the excavations and now approaches its centenary; muted in color by the gray-green of the wild olive, the yellow-green of the pine, the red-brown of the fallen needles, the brown-gray of the tumbled, lichened stones: muted in the mellow sunlight of an empty and memorial peace. On the slope below the treasuries, the breeze from over Mount Kronion sifts fragrance through the pine boughs.

Yet there is a third contemporary impression, by means of which the present can come full circle to the area's most ancient past. Through the centuries, lightning and thunderbolt have riven and shaken Olympia. To be in the grove and the ruins in a night of heavy storm, of pitch-blackness followed by wild white light suddenly splashed on fallen columns, on wet flat stylobates, on the gray reverse sides of the slender raised leaves of olive, is to follow back through time into the old Altis, the grove of primitive altars, where a sense of immanent presence invoked dark sacrifice.

CHAPTER 9 *Places of Prehistory*

O F the classical sites of Greece, while much remains unknown, much can be said with certainty.

Records of persons, places, and events were noted in the course of the daily life of communities that had established measurements of time and space and tools of communication closely enough linked with our own to be readily intelligible.

And as the classical Greeks began to reflect about human institutions, the first historians, political scientists, and philosophers—Herodotus, Thucydides, Xenophon, Demosthenes, Plato, Aristotle—described and commented on the events of their time.

In addition to the sources that are contemporary or near-contemporary with the sites, there are the findings based on the research of our own time, particularly in archaeology, which subject these records to the correction of independent tests.

But while most visitors who come to Greece are primarily concerned with sites of the classical period, other sites from still earlier times have begun to attract almost equal attention.

About these, such contemporary records as exist are either indecipherable or only tentatively interpreted; events are located on a scale of time that is composed of broad approximations. The means of communication with our period, where they exist at all, are the symbols of myth and legend transmitted in an oral tradition that was written down only after long intervals.

Who were the inhabitants of the Greek peninsula who built the tremendous walls that legend attributes to the Cyclops or the Pelasgians, giants of the shadowy past? Engineers of no mean skill, clearly, whose capacity to shape and move huge blocks would remind the viewer of the unknown builders of Stonehenge and the sites of southwest France even without the recent discovery on one of the Stonehenge slabs of the same sign of the double ax that recurs on the structures of Minoan times in Crete.

Two relatively identifiable Aegean civilizations preceded that of historic Greece. The period of the Minoans, whose diverse achievements include the palaces on Crete, goes back perhaps to 3000 B.C.; this people built both the first palaces at Knossos and Phaistos, started around 2000 and destroyed shortly after 1600, and the great centers that replaced them and housed a complex and sophisticated society until an unidentified calamity abruptly enveloped them in earthquake and fire shortly before 1400.

The successors to the Minoans were the Mycenaeans, whose greatest monuments are at Mycenae and Tiryns in the Peloponnese. They likewise left buildings of two distinguishable periods. Their civilization overlapped the Minoan; the time of its pre-eminence was shorter. It was a ruler of Mycenae who gathered the Achaean host for the conflict with Troy that gave the Greek world the greatest of its epics.

The dating, both of the Trojan war and of the successive bards who recounted its episodes, is a prime battleground of scholarship, where specialists who spend their lives among facts and artifacts gladly clash sword on shield, with the mists of the admittedly unknown swirling between them. (The risks of a journalist in such a no man's land are, however, well documented.)

Even in classical times, uncertainties about "Homer" were great enough to produce such epigrams as these from the *Greek Anthology*:

"Who was he that inscribed in pages the war of Troy? or who the long wandering of Laertiades? I find clearly neither his name, nor his city. Heavenly Jove! perhaps Homer has the glory of thy poems!"

> *From Colophon some deem thee sprung;*
> > *From Smyrna some, and some from Chios:*
> *These noble Salamis have sung,*
> > *While those proclaim thee born in Ios;*
> > *And others cry up Thessaly,*
> > *The mother of the Lapithae.*
> > *Thus each to Homer has assign'd*
> > *The birthplace just which suits his mind.*

> *But if I read the volume right,*
> > *By Phoebus to his followers given,*
> *I'd say—They're all mistaken quite,*
> > *And that his real country's heaven;*
> > *While for his mother, she can be*
> > *No other than Calliope.*

Most scholars think the *Iliad* older than the *Odyssey*: dates for the former have been set as early as the mid-tenth century, for the latter as late as the seventh; the odes of the Homeridai—successors to Homer—were composed down into the historic period.

Hesiod is generally regarded as subsequent to Homer, though some authorities place him at the turn of the eighth century. His *Theogony* details the Olympian mythology shared by all of the three separate but related peoples—Aeolians, Ionians, Dorians, who in successive waves, over time, came from the north and settled various areas in Asia Minor, the Islands, the mainland, the Peloponnese. In dialects, particularly in the use of language in the form of literature, in institutions, and in predilections these strains of migrants differed from one another, but they were all Greeks. The legend of Cadmus and the "Sown Men" who sprang from the dragon's teeth conveys the sudden appearances that characterized this obscure time of vast migrations. By around 1000 B.C. they had arrived.

The break between their civilization and that of their predecessors was a sharp one; the contrast is even greater than that between the Etruscans and the Romans, one peninsula to the west. But as more and more becomes known about these earlier peoples, the visitor to the area which used to be thought of as the scene of Greek and Roman "ancient history" views with fascination great works of far older civilizations, in relation to which Greeks and Romans are modern folk indeed.

CHAPTER 10 *The Palaces of Minos*

U NTIL this century, the prehistory of Crete was compounded of legend.

There was the legendary birth of Zeus on the island's 8,000-foot conical peak of Mount Ida. Since titanic Kronos, his father, had heard the prophecy that a son of his would kill time and reign in his stead, he swallowed his children at birth. His consort Rhea, after Demeter, Hera, and Poseidon had been successively swallowed, devised a trick against the time of her next confinement. She gave Kronos a wrapped-up stone to swallow, and bore Zeus secretly on the Cretan mountain, where he was nursed by the goat Amalthea and where the noise of his crying was covered by the shouts of the wild Kouretes as they danced. Later, Zeus fulfilled the ancient prophecy, caused Kronos to vomit up his siblings, then led the battle of gods and titans which ended in his own establishment as head of the Olympian hierarchy.

There was the legend of Zeus' affair with Europa. Transforming himself into a white bull, he swam to Asia Minor and carried away the daughter of the Phoenician king. Of this union was born Minos, who became king of the island, and married Pasiphaë, a daughter of Helios and the nymph Crete.

There was the legend of the Minotaur. Minos dedicated his island to Poseidon, and asked the god to send a white bull up from the sea for sacrifice. The god complied, but the king, struck by the beauty of the animal, kept him for a herd sire and sacrificed a lesser beast. Outraged, Poseidon colluded with Aphrodite to punish Minos; she caused Pasiphaë to fall in love with the white bull. Hidden inside the wooden statue of a cow constructed for her by the artificer Daedalus, she conceived, and bore the Minotaur, half-bull, half-man. Minos concealed the misbegotten monster in a labyrinth; at its center, the annual tribute of youths and maidens which Athens rendered to Minos was sacrificed.

There was the legend of Theseus, who went to Crete to kill the Minotaur. Ariadne, daughter of Minos and Pasiphaë, showed him how to find his way back through the maze, some say by rewinding a ball of thread that he had unrolled on his way in, others, by seeing his way from light reflected by the jewels of a necklace that Dionysus had given to Ariadne. With her, after killing the monster, he started back to Athens. But on the island of Naxos, Dionysus claimed Ariadne for his cult; Theseus returned bringing only a wooden image of Athena that Daedalus had carved.

But the legends left unanswered questions such as these: who were the Minoan people; were they related to the mainland Greeks, or had they come from Africa or the Middle East? What was their language? When did the facts behind the legends actually occur?

Excavations have now provided at least partial answers. Three periods

of Minoan culture, early, middle, and late, have been defined. It was a
Bronze Age culture, ranging in time from about 3000 to about 1100 B.C.
In space, it ranged the Eastern Mediterranean: it had close ties with
Libya, Egypt, the Mesopotamian area, Asia Minor. Another legend re-
counts the love of Minos and two of his brothers for the boy Miletus;
when Miletus preferred one of the brothers and Minos banished the
boy, the lad went to Asia Minor and there founded the city that bore
his name. Similar colonization apparently started other settlements in
Greece proper; the Mycenaean civilization of the Peloponnese and elsewhere is thought to have been the heir of the Minoan world in blood
as well as in time.

Minoan power was based on command of the seas; the empire of the
Minoan kings was a thalassocracy. The island itself was hardly fortified;
sites for the great palaces were selected without military considerations
in mind.

The forces that toppled this civilization were brute contractions in
the island's bowels. Earthquakes are not unknown in Crete even today;
around 1580 B.C. there was a major disaster, and around 1400 B.C. a
holocaust that shook the walls of Minos down.

Very much remains unexplained: why were no bodies of persons
caught in the holocaust found at the sites amid the evidence of activities suspended when half-complete? Was the disaster accompanied by
invasion? Were the great fires started by quakes or by conquerors?

Yet very much has been clarified. Two tremendous palaces and their
surrounding areas have been excavated, at Knossos near Heraklion and
at Phaistos near the south coast and the Libyan Sea; so have several less
extensive settlements, including Hagia Triada near Phaistos and Mallia
and Gournia in eastern Crete.

Comparison of the sites at Knossos and Phaistos underlines the dif-
ferences between excavators who dig with flair and excavators who dig
with care.

163

Sir Arthur Evans, at Knossos at the turn of the century, restored as he went—steel and cement replaced wooden beaming that had burned or turned to powder; painted, peg-pointed columns rose where painted, peg-pointed columns had been before; supplemental frescoes were put over powdered traces beside remaining fragments to fill out the picture; horns of the ever-present bull reappeared where old ones had vanished.

The Italian School, whose work may be watched today at Phaistos, uncovers, sifts, measures, notes, but with minimal exceptions does not restore.

As a result, Phaistos has more verisimilitude, Knossos more drama, with the spectator enjoying it even while knowing that it is only partly real.

At Knossos in August one enters the palace area under an arbor ceilinged with green leaves and down-hanging purple grape clusters. Beyond it a tourist pavilion and shop exhibit Cretan pottery and other handicrafts. Across the fence is a superbly maintained vineyard—the entire area was covered with vines before the excavations began.

Ancient habitation of the spot has been uncovered in at least four major layers. Neolithic man was here, perhaps as far back as 5000 B.C. The beginnings of Bronze Age culture go back to 2600 B.C.; by 2000, a huge palace at Knossos was started, parts of which are the first monuments one sees. A catastrophe destroyed this palace in the early sixteenth century B.C.; the new one begun immediately after this disaster stood until the spring day at the end of the fifteenth century, when the south wind was strong enough to blow almost horizontally across the structure the flames of the second holocaust.

The grandeur of these centuries is stupendous. The highly mannered men who formed this court were accustomed to spacious living: the size of the huge central courtyards, the long connecting corridors, the deep, roof-shaded colonnades supported by massive columns, the broad-treaded stone stairways leading from level to level up and down the slope of the hill were drawn to a scale that the Egyptians had already employed but that would not be used in the West until the age of Imperial Rome.

The Minoan economic base was adequate to sustain this grandeur. Underground storage chambers for oil accommodated perhaps 80,000 gallons. The clay jars or *pithoi* which held not only oil but wine, grain, and dried fruit, were decorated with a rope pattern with numerous loops for handles; found in considerable numbers and amazingly intact, they are taller than a man, the largest ever uncovered. A series of rooms with lead-lined square chests, in which there were fragments of gold leaf, may have been deposit boxes for treasure.

The rooms above the storage chambers were apparently the record rooms of the palace: the clay tablets, some inscribed with hieroglyphs and some with script in Linear A or Linear B writing, were probably preserved by falling into the storey below during the conflagration that consumed the palace, and there being fired to their current hardness.

The Linear A writing has not yet been deciphered. Within the past decade initial success in decoding Linear B was announced by the English architect Michael Ventris; he was killed in a motor accident, however, before his work was definitively established. His translation showed the slabs to be inventories—so many shields, so many spears, so much grain, so many chariots; and censuses—so many men, so many women—rather dull in itself but startling in its indication that the language of the late Minoan records was a form of Greek.

The workrooms of the craftsmen who supplied the court have likewise been identified—in one potter's establishment, a vase was left half-finished.

The sumptuousness of the royal rooms is overwhelming. There were public apartments for religious rites; from the position of shattered sacred vessels, it is thought that a ritual may have been in progress when catastrophe panicked the celebrants. Nearby, in repositories for sacred objects, were found the faïence statues of goddesses handling snakes, now in the Heraklion museum. Pillars were scratched with the symbol of the double ax—the *labrys*—which recurs in stone and in fresco throughout the site. An underground cult of the Mother Goddess, Mistress of Trees and Mountains and Lady of the Wild Animals, was practiced; a jar in the room contained complete equipment for the worship of the domestic snake.

There were public rooms for giving audience—the alabaster high-backed throne of the Kings Minos remains in its millennial position. There is a theater at the northeast corner of the palace grounds, where a royal box fills the angle between two straight-rowed sets of tiered seats.

The private rooms are comparably impressive. The royal apartments are reached by an inner stair, descending from a hall of the guard; the king's are marked with the double ax, the queen's with a sign of the distaff. Light is provided for these chambers below the surface by lustral areas, open-topped vertical shafts that descend along the side of the room to a level below its floor; their white-plastered walls reflect light into the cool and shaded interior. The royal facilities include a bath and flush toilet. A complex system of aqueducts and drains, their terracotta pipes nested at the joints with bevels that speed the flow of water, runs through the entire palace.

But more striking than any other feature of this enormous monument is its wealth of color. Many of the floors, even, have red mortar over their stone slabs; the walls of chamber after chamber are frescoed with the liveliest of drawings and scenes, in vivid and contrasting colors. Even where the decoration is a design rather than a picture, it shows rollicking dolphins, quick fish, shields in bold figure eights.

The scenes of the picture frescoes range over the whole of palace life. Their execution follows certain conventions: the skins of the ladies—their faces, hands, feet, the bare breasts surrounded by the plunging necklines of open blouses—are done in white; the skins of the men in

dark red. Bulls are shown in natural colors, often with spotted hides; other animals are sometimes blue. But the drawing is nowhere stylized—in this regard the contrast could not be greater between parallel presentations of Cretan and Egyptian art.

Minoan architecture is shown in such detail in the frescoes that when Sir Arthur Evans put back some of the pillars of the palace he had ample models from which to draw their proportions. The dress of the people and many of their occupations are exhibited in similar detail.

Each fresco seems to have caught an arrested movement. The "Cup-Bearer" goes actively about his business, displaying the snug cincture and the brief skirt and codpiece worn by men, whose wasp-waistedness is repeated by their figure-eight shields. Their tight, wide belts, perhaps reinforced with metal, contributed to this trimness; they may have been

put on in youth to remain until a loosened acceptance of paunchiness comforted middle age.

The "Ladies in Blue" and "The Parisienne" seem to chatter to music by Offenbach. Their elaborate hairdress with carefully rounded curls lying in black loops against painted cheeks, lavish jewelry, long flounced skirts below open bodices, shown in detail in individual portraits, are repeated en masse in the frescoes of vast numbers of men and women assembled in front of a building, perhaps to witness the bull dance.

The choreography of the bull dance appears in another fresco which catches a boy in the midst of a double somersault onto a bull's back while one girl stands behind the animal to catch him at the end of his leap, and another grips the long plunging horns preparatory to leaping in her turn.

Figures of animals alone are likewise recurrent: the long-tailed griffins couchant, surrounded by saffron plants, in the throne room; a blue, watchful monkey with grave face and sharp eye. Most moving, among animal frescoes, is the dulled suffering of the captured bull, on his fore-knees, head down, tongue out, eyes unseeing.

Two panels display the beauty of the lilies—lilies composed the royal garland of the king.

To reach the other great Minoan palace, at Phaistos, one crosses the island southward. In August, the road runs through pleasant country. Away to the west are the high mountains; in the near view, on either side, are vineyards and garnered grain fields where quickly-running quail thread the stubble. The round threshing floors have been cleared of the harvest; on them, and in the open fields where tall cylinders of butcher's paper have been unrolled in long strips, the villagers are massing grape clusters to dry into raisins in the sun. Here and there, on racks, the best bunches dangle from parallel wire strands running between spaced wooden posts; these will be the table raisins of tomorrow.

Though traversing the valley that leads to the Mesara plain, the road

nevertheless hairpins around a few great gorges; occasionally, among the rocks, stalks of asphodel lift pale lily-flowered cones.

The old peasant men at the village cafés, where wooden tables flank the road so closely as almost to be grazed by the passing bus, grizzle-bearded, booted, black-clad, have weather-worn bronze faces of great dignity.

The bus slowed for a curve as we went through one little settlement. In the dooryard of a modest home, on whose wall an overhanging bough cast a splotch of shadow, I marked a young girl as beautiful as an olive tree. She wore a yellow dress; her lithe body was in the sun, her dark, oval face was profiled against the shadow. Every line and curve expressed close expectation; one could tell she had been listening.

Who on the bus was waiting for this curve also? Quickly, I scanned the passengers: relaxed, inert, every one. Then at the rear, I saw the face of the conductor.

On local Greek buses, incidentally, the conductor is the man in charge. The driver is his subordinate; he is the man who makes the decisions, as starter, information-and-fares authority, bouncer if the passengers quarrel.

The Palaces of Minos

Rather more than halfway to Phaistos is Gortyna, the ancient Gortys, later a Greek settlement, and still later the Roman center of government of both Crete and Cyrenaica.

There, washed by a mill-stream when the archaeologist Frederick Halbherr noted it in 1884, was the curved wall of a Roman odeion, composed of earlier blocks from a Greek building. On it is inscribed a supplement, dating from about 450 B.C., to one of the earliest of written law codes. The code provides working rules for an aristocratic society, with penalties varied according to the status of the offender; it resembles the laws and those that Lycurgus is said to have set for Sparta.

The sea-defended security which made fortification unnecessary is even more evident at Phaistos than at Knossos, for the knoll on which the palace stands slopes gently seaward to both the southeast and the southwest. Pines grow on the knoll east of the palace; I sat there and listened to the wind as it sifted through their boughs, making one sound as it passed the needles, another as it filtered through the cones. The flittering of their segments sounded like a watercourse.

A Greek family came by; since the hazy horizon in both directions might well be water, I was eager to know which was the nearest way to the sea. Mutual gesticulation produced many smiles, but few facts. Suddenly I remembered the story of Xenophon's march to the sea, how he joined the army of Cyrus the younger in his expedition against his brother Artaxerxes II, and after Cyrus' death, when the men were a thousand miles from home and in trouble, how he led them up the Tigris Valley to the shores of the Euxine Sea. When the men saw the water they cried, "Thalassa! Thalassa!" As soon as I said the word, comprehension dawned on my listeners. "Thalassa!" they replied, pointing southwesterly.

The outstanding find at Phaistos was one of the oldest of printed records: the Phaistos disc. This clay disc is covered with spiral bands of hieroglyphs, so far undeciphered. Symbols are grouped by surrounding raised lines; the remarkable thing about them is that each is imprinted in the clay by the pressure of a separate seal stone.

The Phaistos disc is at the museum at Heraklion, along with a collection of seal stones from most of the various Minoan excavations, each worthy of magnified inspection. In addition to the stones there are gold seal rings, many of them with finely designed animal and human figures, jewelry such as the bee pendant from a tomb at Mallia, cut gems of crystal and jasper. There are clay snake goddesses, dove goddesses, a vase collection with motifs of octopus and saffron, endless small bronzes of lively animals. Perhaps the most polished piece is the sacrificial vase in the form of a bull's head from Knossos, in steatite, with long gilded horns, an inset of white shell outlining the muzzle, and eyes of rock crystal rimmed with red jasper.

Here too are very complete collections of funerary chests, painted inside and out in elaborate polychrome, urns, gable-topped boxes.

Upstairs by themselves are the originals of many Knossos frescoes.

Closing hour at the Heraklion museum has one compensation; ejected from the interior, one can sit in the surrounding park and look steeply down on the harbor which the Venetians developed under the name of Candia. As shadows lengthen, a westward walk along the coastal road by the gray-aqua sea leads to the cove that faces a hazy sunset behind Mount Stroumboulas. Supper can be there, or at an outdoor table in the central square near the Venetian fountain.

Afterward, one can move with the crowd through the narrow market streets—past open fruit booths mounded with grapes and melons, open butcher booths hanging with meat from brains to entrails and observed from below by watchful cats, textile booths piled with bolts of cotton cloth, narrow slits with herbs and seeds to offer, wider shops dangling clothes on hangers. It is a bazaar. Crete is part of Greece, but Crete is visibly close to Asia Minor.

CHAPTER 11 *The Mycenaean Citadel*

THE high, wild, desolate landscape of My-
cenae stages the tragic drama of its Atreid kings. Murder, adultery,
madness, a curse transmitted from generation to generation—their story
has been passed down through three millennia, with treatment varying
from Aeschylus to Offenbach.

Atreus and Thyestes were sons of the Pelops who came from Asia
Minor to Arcadia. Thyestes wronged Atreus' wife; in revenge Atreus
killed Thyestes' children and served them to him at a feast. (One boy,
Aegisthus, escaped.) The gods cursed Atreus and his line.

Atreus' sons, Agamemnon and Menelaus, reigned after him, Agamemnon in Mycenae, Menelaus in Sparta. Mycenaean artifacts have
been found as far south as Vaphio below Sparta, and as far west as the

island of Kephalonia, Sicily, and Italy. To the north they have been unearthed in Corinth, Eleusis, Athens, and all the way to Thessaly.

When the Trojan Paris beguiled Menelaus' wife Helen away with him to Asia Minor, Agamemnon was first among peers in the great assemblage of men and ships that gathered before Troy. Homer eulogizes his pre-eminence:

> "Their clans came out like the countless flocks of birds—the geese, the cranes, the long-necked swans—that foregather on the Asian meadow by the streams of Cayster, and wheel about, boldly flapping their wings and filling the whole meadow with harsh cries as they come to ground on an advancing front. So clan after clan poured out from the ships and huts onto the plain of Scamander, and the earth resounded sullenly to the tramp of marching men and horses' hooves, as they found their places in the flowery meadows by the river, innumerable as the leaves and blossoms in their season.
>
> "Thus these long-haired soldiers of Achaea were drawn up on the plain, facing the Trojans with slaughter in their hearts, as many and as restless as the unnumbered flies that swarm round the cowsheds in the spring, when pails are full of milk.
>
> "And now, with the practised ease with which goatherds sort out their wandering flocks when they have mingled in the pastures, the captains brought their companies into battle order; and in among them moved King Agamemnon, with head and eyes like Zeus the Thunderer, with a waist like the War-god's waist, and a breast like Poseidon's. As a bull stands out from the cattle in a herd, conspicuous among the grazing cows, so on that day Zeus made the son of Atreus stand out from the crowd and eclipse his fellow kings."

But when this host assembled in the bay at Aulis, between Attica and the island of Euboia, to sail for Troy, no breeze came. The prophet Calchas declared that Artemis was displeased, and required that for a fair wind, Agamemnon must sacrifice his daughter Iphigeneia. This was done at Artemision; a breeze arose.

Angry at his slaughter of her child, during Agamemnon's nine-year absence at the Trojan war his wife Klytemnestra took his cousin Aegisthus, likewise eager for revenge, as her lover. They determined to kill Agamemnon on his return.

Klytemnestra arranged for a signal of the fall of Troy. To the southeast of the palace at Mycenae is a mountain—the ancient Arachnaion, Hagios Elias today—from which a view sweeps south over the Argos plain, west to Nemea, north all the way to Acrocorinth, and east far out to sea. Klytemnestra stationed a lookout there, and in Aeschylus' *Agamemnon* she recites how, in a single night, the signal came from

> Hephaestus, who cast forth the shining blaze from Ida.
> And beacon after beacon picking up the flare
> carried it here; Ida to the Hermaean horn
> of Lemnos, where it shone above the isle, and next
> the sheer rock face of Zeus on Athos caught it up;
> and plunging skyward to arch the shoulders of the sea
> the strength of the running flare in exultation,
> pine timbers flaming into gold, like the sunrise,
> brought the bright message to Macistus' sentinel cliffs,
> who, never slow nor in the carelessness of sleep
> caught up, sent on his relay in the courier chain,
> and far across Euripus' streams the beacon flare
> carried to signal watchmen on Massapion.
> These took it again in turn, and heaping high a pile
> of silvery brush flamed it to throw the message on.
> And the flare sickened never, but grown stronger yet
> outleapt the river valley of Asopus like
> the very moon for shining, to Cithaeron's scaur
> to waken the next station of the flaming post.

These watchers, not contemptuous of the far-thrown blaze,
kindled another beacon vaster than commanded.
The light leaned high above Gorgopis' staring marsh,
and striking Aegyplanctus' mountain top, drove on
yet one more relay, lest the flare die down in speed.
Kindled once more with stintless heaping force, they send
the beard of flame to hugeness, passing far beyond
the promontory that gazes on the Saronic strait
and flaming far, until it plunged at last to strike
the steep rock of Arachnus near at hand, our watchtower.
And thence there fell upon this house of Atreus' sons
the flare whose fathers mount to the Idaean beacon.
These are the changes on my torchlight messengers,
one from another running out the laps assigned.
The first and the last sprinters have the victory.
By such proof and such symbol I announce to you
my lord at Troy has sent his messengers to me.

So when Agamemnon returned, his wife and her lover were prepared to murder him. Trojan Cassandra, Priam's daughter whom Agamemnon had brought back with him as his slave and spoil of war, foretells the further course of the tragedy.

As Cassandra foresaw, Electra and Orestes, the remaining children of the royal couple, determine to kill their mother and her lover to avenge their father's death. After these murders, Orestes is pursued by the Furies, though at the end of the *Oresteia* trilogy Aeschylus has Athena intervene to lay the curse and turn the Furies from Erinnyes bent on vengeance to Eumenides moved to mercy.

The stones of Mycenae neither confirm nor deny this legend, but they bear witness that a mighty dynasty once ruled this land. Indeed, there seems to have been a sequence of two separate dynasties, the evidence being offered by the differing methods of burial found in two groups of royal graves. Legend supports the indication of two dynasties: while the version given by Apollodorus and the stories repeated by Pausanias vary rather widely, they are in accord in designating Perseus as the original founder of the city. The Perseid dynasty was then followed by the Pelopids.

The first extensive citadel on this rock 900 feet above the sea is thought to have been built and occupied during the years 1700–1400 when Minoan culture in Crete was at its height; an interconnection between the two civilizations shows in the similarity of their artifacts.

The tombs of this dynasty are shaft graves, outside the first but included within the enlarged confines of the second citadel. There were six of them, containing nineteen skeletons and ten steles; five were found in the original grave circle and one was located only within the past decade under a later house by the Lion Gate. In the first group, Heinrich Schliemann unearthed his kings and queens, laid away in sumptuous state and masked in gold.

Seventeen hundred years before, Pausanias had written:

"Among the ruins of Mycenae is a conduit called Persea and there are underground buildings of Atreus and his children, where their treasures were kept. There is a grave of Atreus and graves of all those who on their return from Ilium with Agamemnon were murdered by Aegisthus after a banquet which he gave them. The tomb of Cassandra is disputed: the Lacedaimonians of Amyclae claim that it is at Amyclae. Another tomb is that of Agamemnon; another is that of Euremydon the charioteer; another is that of Teledamus and Pelops. The two last are said to have been twin children of Cassandra, who were murdered by Aegisthus in their infancy, after he had murdered their parents. . . . But Clytemnestra and Aegisthus were buried a little distance from the wall; for they were deemed unworthy to be buried within the walls, where Agamemnon himself and those who had been murdered with him were laid."

This hearsay passed on by Pausanias seemed doubly verified when Schliemann not only unearthed royal tombs in the first citadel's grave-yard, but found others outside its walls. He telegraphed the Greek King:

"With extreme joy I announce to Your Majesty that I have dis-covered the tombs which tradition, echoed by Pausanias, has designated as the sepulchres of Agamemnon, Cassandra, Eurymedon and all their companions who were killed while partaking of a meal with Clytem-nestra and her lover Aegisthus. They were surrounded with a double circle of stone slabs, which would not have been erected unless they were great personages. In the tombs I found immense treasures of the most ancient objects of pure gold.

"These treasures alone will fill a great museum, the most wonderful in the world, and for centuries to come thousands of foreigners will flock to Greece to see them. . . ."

But Pausanias' references actually covered two dynasties, two palaces, two sets of royal tombs. The graves found by Schliemann in and near the first citadel may actually have contained the dynasty that preceded the Atreides, ruling during the time of the Minoan kings. The new line of Mycenaean rulers, who came to power after the Cretan cataclysm, and practiced different burial customs, were more probably those who headed the expedition to bring war to Troy.

The second citadel, which they built after 1400, greatly enlarged the previously defended area with new encircling walls of huge blocks of stone. Their massive inner gate, at the end of a stone-faced passage, is framed by four monoliths; a fifth forms a curved lintel 15 feet across. In a triangle above the lintel, standing lionesses confront each other on either side of a peg-pointed pillar that looks as though it had been taken directly from the palace at Knossos. The Minoan symbol of the double ax is likewise repeated in the scene of an offering to the Mother God-

178

dess carved in the most beautiful of the signet rings that Schliemann found.

The entrance leads past a porter's lodge and second gate beside the earlier royal graveyard.

The royal palace—megaron, throne room, porticoes, private quarters—tops the rise; as in Knossos, some of the floors are of painted plaster, and even today there are traces of frescoes on the walls. From the neighboring palace of Tiryns, reputed home of Herakles, a fresco of a boar hunt, much damaged and now in the Athens museum, shows two boars, harried by five spotted dogs and attacked by four men and one woman with spears; the feeling of its design is the same as that of the inlaid sword handles discovered at Mycenae.

The citadel had an assured water supply: at the northeast corner of the acropolis, a large subterranean stairway with carefully cut steps leads sharply down through the rock to a reservoir, 40 feet below, which is fed by an outside spring.

The tombs of the kings of the second palace were located at some distance from the citadel; they were enormous beehives cut into the rock. That known as the Treasury of Atreus is the most elaborate: at the end of an avenue sliced into the hill, its vertical sides faced with huge slabs, is a doorway linteled by a block weighing some hundred and twenty tons. Above this is a triangular space, left to lighten the load and divert the stress; it was formerly masked by a slab with carved designs in rosso antico marble. The plinths forming the sides of the frame were adorned by half-columns of gray-green limestone. Both the British Museum and the Archaeological Museum in Athens have fragments of each of these decorations.

Inside is a rotunda close to fifty feet across; its ceiling is a dome formed by fitted stone blocks; the circular stone that forms the lid is some forty feet above floor level. A small room cut out from the side of the rotunda is thought to be the sepulchral chamber of the head of the family; the other bodies would have been laid in the rotunda itself. This tomb, and some of the others so far opened, had been pillaged long before the age of archaeology.

Unlike the Minoan civilization, the Mycenaean era did not come to an abrupt halt. The invading Dorians of the Iron Age burned the palaces at Mycenae and at Tiryns, but though Argos became the important city of the area the walled heights remained peopled into the historic period.

In its diminished existence, Mycenae furnished a modest quota of men to resist the Persians in the fighting at Plataeia; the name Mykanes is inscribed on the tripod; erected at Delphi in honor of this victory, that stands today where Justinian re-erected it, in the Hippodrome at Istanbul.

But in the year of that victory, the Argives, who had opposed sending help to fight the Persians because their arch-enemy Sparta was promoting the campaign, turned on the Mycenaean citadel and devastated it.

By the time Pausanias saw it, its desolation was almost as complete as it is today.

CHAPTER 12 *Waves of Conquest*

PHILIP of Macedon's victory at Chaironeia in 338 B.C., and his formation thereafter of a new league in which he was the dominant partner, forced Greece into the inclusive political structure that its city-states had been unable to achieve in freedom.

The inbred particularism which the city-state inculcated in its citizens is exemplified by the oath required of the youth of Dreros and Knossos in Crete with regard to neighboring Lyktos, of which an inscription remains:

"This is the oath of the young men not yet of age for military service, to the number of a hundred and eighty:

182

Waves of Conquest

I swear by Hestia of the Prytaneium, by Zeus Agoraios, Zeus Tallaios, by Delphinian Apollo, by Athena, Guardian of the city, by Pythian Apollo, by Leto, by Artemis, by Ares, by Aphrodite, by Hermes, by the Sun, by Britomartis, by Phoenix, by Amphiona, by Earth and Heaven, by Heroes male and female, by springs and rivers and all gods male and female that I will never bear good will towards the men of the city of Lyttos in any act or plan of mine, either by night or by day, and I will contrive evil as far as in me lies against the city of the men of Lyttos.

Division so deep, embittered by internecine wars, invited engulfment. From the successful Greek resistance to the Persians in 490 and 480 B.C. to defeat by the Macedonians in 338, the time span was only a hundred and fifty years.

And in less than two hundred further years, a second conquest permanently overlaid the Macedonian hegemony; thereafter, Greece was administered first as one, later as two provinces of Rome.

These conquests eliminated Greek autonomous politics and ended Greek military power. But Greek civilization, transmitted though it often was by men in subject or slave status, in turn went far toward conquering its conquerors east and west: Hellenism spread under foreign empires further than the Hellenes alone had been able to spread it as free men.

The first conqueror, Philip of Macedon, had been thoroughly Hellenized during three years spent as a hostage at Thebes at a time when Thebes, after the battle of Leuctra, had assumed from Sparta the hegemony which Sparta took from Athens at the end of the Peloponnesian Wars. Philip's son Alexander had Aristotle as a tutor; their Athenian contemporaries were Plato and Demosthenes.

Since Persia, ever looking for new Greek openings, had been a Spartan ally in the recent wars, Philip proposed reconquest of the Persian-held cities of Asia Minor. His son Alexander, succeeding to the throne at the

age of twenty, had larger ideas still: with Greek armies and Greek generals he subdued all of Persia, burned Persepolis, adopted the dress and ceremonial of the Persian kings, and continued his conquest to the borders of India.

Alexander's death at Babylon at the age of thirty-three, and the subsequent tripartite division of his empire among his generals, disjointed his grand design. But Greek cities, Greek settlers, and Greek mercenaries impregnated Western Asia with Hellenized architecture and Hellenized art; its magnificence endures in the sarcophagus representing Alexander hunting, now at Istanbul, and the altar of Zeus at Pergamon. In Egypt, an intellectual life that was Greek in origin was maintained for a thousand years from the foundation of Alexandria to the Arab conquest of A.D. 643.

A similar Greek impact is equally visible in Rome.

In Greece itself, there was a gradual decline. The architectural and artistic marks of the Roman period are many; diminished in quality, they form a more or less continuous sequence with what had gone before. The debasement of art was the result of a combination of mass production and a taste comparable to that expressed in the nineteenth century municipal art of the West. In Roman times, memorial statues could be ordered from stock, with heads in the likeness of the subject added to prefabricated bodies—there are some in the museum at Olympia.

Statues emphasized naturalism, with draperies approaching the frilly when draperies were used, and bodies approaching the fleshy when draperies were omitted.

Triumphal arches, like the one built when Hadrian came to Athens, were an innovation; so were monumental public baths. Enlargements of Greek facilities—the Roman agora in Athens, the palaestra at Olympia—and rebuilding of razed cities—Corinth and Patras—went on, but in general what was done was not something new but merely something less good than what had been done before, constructed on a dwindling economic base.

During the last years of the Roman Republic, Greece supplied a number of decisive battlegrounds for Roman struggles: in 48 B.C. Caesar defeated Pompey at Pharsala in Thessaly; in 42, Octavius and Anthony defeated Brutus and Cassius at Philippi in Thrace; in 31, Octavian defeated Anthony—Cleopatra was there, too—in the west-coast harbor of Actium. But Greece itself lived in a backwater of history.

Over the next period, the events which had the largest subsequent effect on the Greek future appeared very small indeed. In the Roman province of Judea, a new religion acquired a small number of devoted believers. In the decade of the 50's A.D. one of these, Paul, himself a convert from Jewish orthodoxy, undertook a preaching mission to the Greek cities in Asia Minor, Macedonia, and Achaia.

The movement caused little stir at the time. But later, as Christianity became formally organized and as its converts in high places increased to include the Roman Emperor himself, as religious dogma and the hierarchy of the organized church became factors in the politics and economics of imperial power, old institutions were effaced in Greece, and the new religion spread its doctrines, art, and architecture there.

The change was accelerated after Constantine, in A.D. 330, moved the capital of the empire to Byzantium; succeeding emperors both suppressed Greek customs and adopted Greek ways.

In A.D. 393 the Emperor Theodosius I, as part of a campaign against paganism, put an end to the Olympic Games; the fourth century also saw the end of the Delphic oracle. The old gods retreated to mountain fastnesses, though their hold on the people was not wholly broken. In 529, the Emperor Justinian closed the philosophic academies of Athens.

At the same time, the development of Christian theology was greatly influenced by Greek philosophy. The early gospels were known through

Greek texts. In A.D. 627 Greek was formally recognized, and Latin discarded, as the official language of the Eastern Church.

Later still, when the feudal societies of Western Europe became forceful realities and old imperial power waned, waves of Western conquest washed the shores of Greece. The Crusaders, initiating military undertakings to free the Holy Places from the infidel, overran the intervening areas on both island and mainland Greece.

But the force of this tide also slackened and reversed. Jerusalem was lost in 1291. In 1453, the Turks captured Constantinople and almost immediately overran the Greek peninsula, absorbing Latin duchies and Greek despotates alike. Greece was thereafter in the grip of Asian absolutism. With flickerings of revolt, it remained so until the Age of Enlightenment revived in the Western world the political philosophy of the fifth century. The sequence of democratic revolutions beginning in America in 1776 and France in 1789, induced by the renewed interest in man, freedom, and the democratic state, included the wars of liberation from which, in the 1820's, Greece re-emerged as an independent and united nation. Little by little, through the nineteenth and twentieth centuries, through abortive revolts, the Balkan Wars, World War I and World War II, outlying Greek areas were reclaimed. The expulsion of the Asia Minor Greeks by the Turks in 1921–1922 represented a final foreign conquest of the ancient eastern Aegean cities, but Epirus and Thrace, Crete, Corfu, and, at the end of World War II, the Dodecanese, were reunited with Greece, and in the remaining area of nationalistic unrest, Cyprus, an accommodation appears to have been arranged recently.

These millennial waves of conquest all left deposits; today's traveler, even though he may come primarily because of interest in the Greek classical world, finds arresting evidence of their passing in mighty monuments.

CHAPTER 13 *Early Christians*

THE Apostle Paul arrived in Corinth in A.D. 51–52. He came from Athens, where he had just startled the marketplace tellers of new things by preaching on the Areopagus about the Unknown God.

The city which he saw after crossing the Isthmus, with few exceptions other than its temple of Apollo, had been built from the ground up within the memory of its oldest inhabitants, for during the hundred years after 146 B.C., Corinth had had no history because the city did not exist.

As early as 218 B.C., Rome had begun to contest the Macedonian control of Greece. In 194, at the Isthmian Games, Rome announced the "liberation" of the Greeks; but this independence proved transitory.

Early Christians

Complete defeat of the Macedonians established Roman rule in 168.

In 146, however, Greeks and Macedonians together attempted to throw off the Roman yoke; Corinth was the center of resistance. So, as soon as the rebellion was crushed, the Roman general Mummius deleted the city from the map with a thoroughness comparable to the parallel treatment of Carthage.

It was not until a hundred years later that Julius Caesar declared that both Corinth and Carthage should be repopulated. Settlers were sent out from Italy. Then, under Augustus, Corinth became the seat of government from which the Roman Proconsul of Achaia administered most of ancient Greece.

The city quickly resumed its historic function as the entrepôt of Mediterranean trade. The ports on each side of the Isthmus of Corinth, Cenchreae to the east and Lechaeum to the west, provided for transshipment overland of cargoes destined for east-west trade; this was both safer and speedier than the long voyage around the capricious capes of the southern Peloponnese.

Recently-found roadways with tracks show that even galleys themselves, lightened of their loads, were dragged across the Isthmus. Indeed, the idea of cutting a canal across this 4-mile spine of rock was repeatedly considered. It had attracted Alexander the Great—Pausanias remarks that it was his only undertaking that did not succeed; the Knidians entertained it until warned off by the Delphic oracle; at the time of Nero's state visit work was actually started, then abandoned; Herodes Atticus weighed the project; but it was accomplished only in A.D. 1882–1893.

The high stoa which formed the south side of the Corinthian agora, and which Caesar's colonists restored according to the original plan, was perhaps the largest in Greece; its 531-foot length accommodated government offices and a double row of thirty-three shops.

In front of this stoa, flanked by a further row of shops, from which

steps descend at intervals to the level of the Agora, was the Bema, the
judgment seat where offenders were brought before the Roman Proconsul—his name was Gallio, in St. Paul's time—for judgment.

Many of the shops in the south stoa can be identified as taverns by
their 39-foot well shafts, connected with the Peirene spring, in which
they cooled drinks. This famous spring was thought to have two outlets. One was on the acropolis of Acrocorinth, the height behind the
city. One was on the plain; its waters supplied the fountain at the
northeast corner of the Agora.

Here of an evening the city's celebrated courtesans gathered; their
beauty was renowned; their price gave rise to the proverb that not every
merchant can afford to go to Corinth. Of them all, Lais was accounted
the loveliest. Plato made an epigram of the story of how she shrank
from growing old:

> *I Lais, once of Greece the pride,*
> *For whom so many suitors sigh'd,*
> *Now aged grown, at Venus's shrine*
> *The mirror of my youth resign;*
> *Since what I am, I will not see;*
> *And what I was, I cannot be.*

Pausanias notes that her tomb was marked by a statue of a lioness
holding a ram in her forepaws; Antipater of Sidon wrote as her epitaph:

"I contain her who in Love's company luxuriated in gold and purple,
more delicate than tender Cypris, Lais the citizen of sea-girt Corinth,
brighter than the white waters of Pirene; that mortal Cytherea who had
more noble suitors than the daughters of Tyndareus, all plucking her
mercenary favors. Her very tomb smells of sweet-scented saffron; her
bones are still soaked with fragrant ointment, and her anointed locks
still breathe a perfume as of frankincense. For her Aphrodite tore her

lovely cheeks, and sobbing Love groaned and wailed. Had she not made her bed the public slave of gain, Greece would have battled for her as for Helen."

Into this teeming worldliness, St. Paul came to preach the gospel of Christ. The *Book of Acts* gives an account of his mission:

"After these things Paul departed from Athens, and came to Corinth; and found a certain Jew named Aquila, born in Pontus, lately come from Italy with his wife Priscilla; (because that Claudius had commanded all Jews to depart from Rome:) and came unto them. And because he was of the same craft, he abode with them, and wrought: for by their occupation they were tent-makers.

"And he reasoned in the synagogue every sabbath, and persuaded the Jews and the Greeks.

"And when Silas and Timotheus were come from Macedonia, Paul was pressed in the spirit, and testified to the Jews that Jesus was Christ. And when they opposed themselves, and blasphemed, he shook his raiment, and said unto them, Your blood be upon your own heads; I am clean: from henceforth will I go unto the Gentiles.

"And he departed thence, and entered into a certain man's house, named Justus, one that worshipped God, whose house joined hard to the synagogue.

"And Crispus, the chief ruler of the synagogue, believed on the Lord and all his house; and many of the Corinthians hearing believed, and were baptized.

"Then spake the Lord to Paul in the night by a vision, Be not afraid, but speak, and hold not thy peace: For I am with thee, and no man shall set on thee to hurt thee: for I have much people in this city. And he continued there a year and six months, teaching the word of God among them.

"And when Gallio was the deputy of Achaia, the Jews made insurrection with one accord against Paul, and brought him to the judgment seat, Saying, This fellow persuadeth men to worship God contrary to the law.

"And when Paul was now about to open his mouth, Gallio said unto the Jews, If it were a matter of wrong, or wicked lewdness, O ye Jews, reason would that I should bear with you: But if it be a question of words and names, and of your law, look ye to it; for I will be no judge of such matters. And he drave them from the judgment seat.

"Then all the Greeks took Sosthenes, the chief ruler of the synagogue, and beat him before the judgment seat. And Gallio cared for none of these things."

Read against this background, St. Paul's two subsequent letters to the Christians at Corinth take on the reality of a personal correspondence. Struggles of factions within the newly-formed church, uncertainties as to what is proper for Christians in relation to heathen religious practices and in respect to orthodox Jews, difficulty in distinguishing between religious experience and the emotional excesses of "speaking with tongues," occurrences of weaknesses of the flesh among the faithful, all the problems he discusses occurred in an area bounded by the Bema, the Peirene fountain, the temple of Apollo, and the theater which the Romans rebuilt in order to add gladiatorial combats to the existing brutality of this big port town.

It was people living in the midst of this corruption whom he assured:

"For this corruptible must put on incorruption, and this mortal must put on immortality. So when this corruptible shall have put on incorruption, and this mortal shall have put on immortality, then shall be brought to pass the saying that is written, Death is swallowed up in victory. O death, where is thy sting? O grave, where is thy victory? The sting of death is sin: and the strength of sin is the law. But thanks be to God, which giveth us the victory through our Lord Jesus Christ."

And it was to these people that he preached charity:

"Though I speak with the tongues of men and of angels, and have
not charity, I am become as sounding brass, or a tinkling cymbal. And
though I have the gift of prophecy, and understand all mysteries, and
all knowledge; and though I have all faith, so that I could remove
mountains, and have not charity, I am nothing. And though I bestow
all my goods to feed the poor, and though I give my body to be burned,
and have not charity, it profiteth me nothing."

A collection of artists' concepts through the ages of the revelation
recorded by St. John on the island of Patmos would make a fascinating
exhibition.

It would range from Giotto's flat little island, just big enough to
hold the prophet and his oversize inkstand, and the wing of Memling's
triptych of the Mystical Marriage of St. Catherine which shows the
evangelist under a sky filled with his visions, to the fantasy of the tapestries recently restored to the walls inside the ramparts of the Château
d'Angers, which give in woven detail the whole sequence of his descriptions, from the seven angels with the seven vials to the beast with the
seven heads and the ten horns and ten crowns upon the horns. It would
include Dürer's gaunt horsemen and the present replacements of the
wooden statues of Gog and Magog destroyed in London's Guildhall fire
in World War II.

And in an exhibition where anachronism would be practically a con-
dition of admission, surely one entry might be vouchsafed present-day
Patmos itself.

The steamers that call there ply between the Peiraeus and Rhodes.
If the stop is made on the return voyage, the boat sails by daylight past
the whole sequence of Dodecanese islands: past Kos, where Hippocra-
tes carried on his work of healing, and where the enormous plane tree,
still alive though heavily supported by pillared reinforcements, is said

to have shaded him at his work; past Kalymnos, home of sponge fishermen; past the fringe of little islands along the Asia Minor shore.

Then, in the late afternoon, on the northwestern horizon, so far away that the land supporting it does not show at all, appears a shining city like a mirage above the waters:

"And I saw a new heaven and a new earth: for the first heaven and the first earth were passed away; and there was no more sea.

"And I John saw the holy city, new Jerusalem, coming down from God out of heaven, prepared as a bride adorned for her husband.

"And I heard a great voice out of heaven saying, Behold, the tabernacle of God is with men, and he will dwell with them, and they shall be his people, and God himself shall be with them, and be their God.

"And God shall wipe away all tears from their eyes; and there shall be no more death, neither sorrow, nor crying, neither shall there be any more pain: for the former things are passed away.

"And he that sat upon the throne said, Behold I make all things new. And he said unto me: Write; for these words are true and faithful. . . .

"And the city had no need of the sun, neither of the moon, to shine in it: for the glory of the Lord did lighten it, and the Lamb is the light thereof."

As the ship comes closer, the white-crowned island pushes up from the sea. Its deeply indented harbor town of Scala—a market place and cluster of houses with patterned pebble courtyard floors—appears at the water's edge. But above, back-lighted from the westering sun beyond the blackening brown of the near hill, 700 feet higher than the sea, the vision we had seen earlier remained.

Where the sunlight still colored their far edges, its white walls were indeed as of jasper; the side toward us was purpled with the Hellenic afterglow. At its apex, the five bronze bells in the open belfry hung against a zenith that was still bright blue.

195

What matters if this representation of St. John's vision is an anachronism? What matters that in his time, except for a disused pagan
altar, the mountaintop was bare?

St. John is said to have recorded his revelation in a cave, now a sanctuary, something more than halfway up the mile-long ascent to the

upper town. It was almost exactly a thousand years after his exile from Rome to this island that the mountaintop monastery which now bears his name was founded; in A.D. 1088 the Greek emperor gave the island to St. Christodulos so that he might establish it.

Over the centuries, the buildings around the monastery were augmented: the Venetians captured Patmos in 1207; after the fall of Constantinople, it received numerous refugees.

By the latter part of the seventeenth century, a theological seminary attracted students from many lands; the library of the monastery contains priceless manuscripts, Byzantine, Frankish, Turkish, including a gospel according to St. Mark of the fifth century on purple vellum, illuminated in gold and silver.

From roofs and ramparts, one looks down in all directions across the purple sea. The Venetians under Morosini did so, with confidence. In the confused days of pirate incursions, the monks did so, in fear. Today, the scene is as peaceful and domestic as the fragrant pots of thyme that decorate the doorsteps along the steep passageways, fondled by caressing hands as visitors descend from the holy city back to their waiting ship.

St. John's revelation shows the impingement on Christian thinking of a long literature of apocalyptic prophecy; the letters of St. Paul show the impact of the world upon the newly-forming Christian church. Similarly, the new religion found an architecture expressive of its purpose in an environment of pagan styles.

The tremendous ecclesiastical building programs of the Emperor Justinian did much to set the Eastern Orthodox pattern. They ranged from the mosaics depicting himself and the Empress Theodora at S. Vitale in Ravenna to his basilica and hospital in Jerusalem, but Hagia Sophia—Santa Sophia—in Constantinople was his master monument.

The dome had long been known in the architecture of the Middle East; the Romans adopted and developed it for use in baths and in temples—Baiae near Naples and the Pantheon in Rome are early examples. But the scale of the new domed church built in Constantinople between A.D. 532 and 537 was new indeed, and its centrality to Eastern Christendom made it the model for the more modest churches of which many remain in Greece as monuments of Byzantine art.

The very smallest churches—some of the island chapels, for instance— have only a single dome, built on pendentives springing from the walls of a square. Most churches have a larger central dome, often raised on a drum to give it pre-eminence, surrounded by smaller domes, with half- domes at the apse or at the ends of aisles.

The usual plan of a church provides an atrium at the west front, occasionally developed as a cloister with a phiale, or fount for ablutions, in its center. A vestibule or narthex, sometimes treated as an open porch like a stoa, sometimes incorporated as a hall in the interior of the build- ing, shelters arriving worshipers. Doors open from the narthex into the naos or nave, the gathering place of the faithful.

At the eastern end of the naos is an ikonostasis, a high screen, often handsomely carved, on which ikons are displayed; it separates the area of the laity from the area reserved for the clergy. It frequently has three doors; through the center, or holy door, the altar is visible.

The ambon, or pulpit, is in front of the ikonostasis; in more elaborate churches, a solea, corresponding to the choir of a Western structure, is set off by a balustrade of wood or stone and may contain two ambons, one for reading the gospel and one for preaching.

Behind the ikonostasis, and between it and the altar, is the bema, the clergy's area, usually with a raised floor; this space may also contain a bishop's cathedra. The altar area is often covered by a ciborium, a square, arched roof supported by four columns. In the great churches, the ciborium was ornately carved; occasionally it was made of silver.

If the church has side aisles, at their eastern ends the left of the lat- eral apses is used as a prothesis for the preparation of the elements, the right as a deaconicon or robing room.

The outside of Orthodox churches is plain: the approaching worshiper sees red roof tiles, tan walls, the black accent of an occasional cypress tree. But inside, decoration and color are everywhere; their richness and intricacy recall the textiles of India, the carpets of Persia. Pavements are often inlaid, side walls veneered with colored marble; vaults and domes are frescoed or inlaid with mosaic. Surviving examples show that the vestments of the Byzantine clergy expressed in fabric the same colorful magnificence.

Light falls on this brilliance from circuits or crowns of windows that pierce the bases of the domes.

Neither statues nor reliefs are used in Orthodox churches; the Bible stories are conveyed by paintings and mosaics; ikons are the only images.

There was a special reason for this. To all early Christians, the affirmation of monotheism in the first commandment, and the warning against fetishism in the second, were central to their faith, but to Greek early Christians, living in a world of polytheism where magnificent graven images in life-sized marble and bronze were on every hand, the issue of image-worship was exceptionally real. Hence their attacks on paganism not infrequently included physical destruction; justification could be found in *Exodus* 23, verse 24:

"Thou shalt not bow down to their gods, nor serve them, nor do after their works; but thou shalt utterly overthrow them, and quite break down their images."

Even among Christians, allegations of image-worship flared in the Iconoclast controversy that shook the Eastern Church in the eighth and ninth centuries, until the Empress Irene, herself a Greek, dispelled the fervor of the Iconoclasts and became an Orthodox saint.

But while images were absent, mosaics or frescoes covered the vaulting of almost every church. The mosaics are made of imbedded minute pieces of vividly colored glass—green, blue, red—usually with a gold background to give harmony from vault to vault. Whitewashed over when churches were converted into mosques under the Turks, now being revealed again by delicate removal of overlay, more and more of these jewels, at Hagia Sophia and at churches in all parts of Greece, are visible from year to year.

Greek Byzantine art appears at its undisputed best in the Mount Athos monasteries, in the frescoes of the churches at Mistra, and the mosaics of Hosios Lukas in Phocis and the church at Daphni on the road between Athens and Eleusis. But beyond these, each traveler ac-

quires vividly defended individual attachments elsewhere, and the process of restoration constantly widens his opportunities for choice.

Startling, at first sight, are the eyes of Byzantine saints. Look up at
the apex of a central dome: the great eyes of the Pantokrator (Christ)
seem affixed on you, only you, with terrible intensity. Black outlined,
very white of cornea and very black of pupil, they are drawn large beyond the proportions of the usual face; a first reaction finds them unreal. Yet in any Greek crowd there are usually two or three people with
Byzantine eyes.

I saw such eyes first at the taffrail of the ferry that plies between
Antipatras and Patras at the western end of the Corinthian Gulf. She
was a young girl, sixteen or seventeen, and she looked unhappy. She was
alone.

All day, I had been driving down from Epirus, through a land of
grinding poverty where Homer's phrase about "bright-eyed hunger" had
been in my mind.

I asked the passenger next to me to ask her if I might take her picture, and would she like me to mail her a print if it was good? Here is
her letter, translated by the English-speaking daughter of her employer,
that tells the story of the girl with Byzantine eyes:

"I thank you very much for your polite act, to send me the photo.
I wanted, very much, the day that I met you, to open to you my heart
and to tell you my small story and everything about me. But unhappily
I did not know English so I couldn't tell you anything.

"But now I wrote the letter in Greek and another girl translated it.

"My good madame I hope Greece was beautiful to your eyes and
to come back quickly to visit it another time. I like very much my
country. It is poor, it is small, but it is the place that I saw for the
first time the light of day. The everyone's country is lovely.

"Do you want now to tell you something about me? Yes? Then I
begin.

"I am born in a small village of Epiros, two days, by foot, from the town of Arta. I am the third child of my family, in which there are still six children. My father is cultivator but our village hasn't water, the spring is far, and so if good God brings rain, well, if no we cannot collect still the seed. Then the winter comes, the snow covers all things and the cruel hunger beats the door of our miserable small houses.

"When I was very young I didn't understand anything of all these. But after a little time, when I understood our situation I was twelve years old. Our misery made me take a grand resolution. I asked from my father to go away in Athens to work.

"So I kissed many times my small brothers and sisters, my sweet mother, my father and with the eyes full of tears that I separate all them, I came in Athens.

"I help a family. Happily it is a very good family. I work much but never mind. I earn my bread and I am content.

"Last year that I met you I had visited my parents. They are better now with a mouth less. . . ."

CHAPTER 14 *Crossroads of the Crusaders*

T HE Fourth Crusade started with a detour, an expedition initiated by the Venetians to restore Alexius Comnenus to the imperial Byzantine throne. The Christian warriors took Constantinople on July 18, 1203, established the new emperor. But Alexius proved unable to deliver the rewards that his European backers had anticipated. So the following year the victors deposed him, dividing the spoils and justifying their action to the Roman Pope on the grounds that they had subjugated a schismatic people.

They made Baldwin of Flanders emperor, and Thomas Morosini of Venice patriarch of the Church. Quickly, other participants in the expedition occupied adjacent territories, carved out principalities and dukedoms, established feudal rule.

In Greece, Boniface of Montferrat took Thessalonika, marched to Athens and Corinth, awarded Athens as a duchy to the Burgundian family of de la Roche. Argos and Corinth became a lordship under Leo Sguros.

The Venetians, quickly spotting the best positions for trade, occupied Durazzo on the coast of Epirus, Modon and Coron in the Peloponnese, the islands of Crete and Euboia; the Doge remarked that they now ruled "a quarter and a half of the Greek Empire."

In the Islands, feudal nomenclature designated the Grand Duchy of Lemnos, the Duchy of Naxos, the Lordship of Santorin, the Marquisate of Origo. Only in Rhodes did a Greek—Gabalas—establish a despotate.

In the Peloponnese, the principality of Achaia or Morea became the possession of two Champagnards, Guillaume de Champlitte, who shortly returned to France, and Geoffroi de Villehardouin, who held it alone thereafter, and whose sons succeeded him.

On the mainland, the sole remaining Greek enclave was in Epirus, under Michaelangelo, an illegitimate son of the Comnenus family. At first, his despotate reached only from Naupactus to Durazzo, but it served him as a base from which to rival the claims of the imperial court set up at Nicaea in 1203 by the survivors of the debacle at Constantinople.

The new occupiers were not the first Latins to make conquests in Greece; Athens had known them at the time of the First Crusade. Some of the new tenures were temporary; the Nicaean Empire shortly recovered the islands of the Asia Minor littoral, Thrace, and Thessalonika; and the despot of Epirus obtained Crete and Rhodes. Many of the other placed changed hands among Franks, Catalans, Sicilians, Aragonese, Venetians, Genoese.

Yet over wide areas in Greece during the thirteenth century, European ways of life prevailed. Athens and Andravida, the Morean capital in the western Peloponnese, were French-speaking centers of chivalry that according to contemporary chroniclers rivaled the brilliance of feudalism in the West. The *Chronicle of Morea* describes a tournament held in Corinth in 1305: its account of the grace of the chevaliers, the caparisons of their horses, the polish of their armor, the color of their banners, the protocol and the precedence of their entry into the lists follows a pattern familiar to troubadors of the courts of Richard Coeur de Lion and Saint Louis.

From Acrocorinth in the north to Maina and Monemvasia in the south, from Klemoutsi in the west to the Kastro of Larissa at Argos, the crenelated walls of enduring Gothic fortifications rose against the skyline in a surge of building reminiscent of that in Britain in the years just after the Norman conquest. Klemoutsi, incidentally, is a corruption of the French Clair Mont, the cloudless mountain. Its nearby port, called Clarentza, became the source of the title of the English Duke of Clarence who died in a butt of malmsey, and the malmsey itself took its name from a corruption of Monemvasia.

But Andravida, a city like the background of a medieval painting with its Gothic cathedral, whose choir still stands, its church of the Templars, its Carmelite monastery, its seat of Frankish parliaments, was not the Villehardouins' only citadel.

Another was at Mistra, across the Eurotas River from the site of ancient Sparta. There, just east of the Taygetas range, on a hill whose western edge plummets into the dark, Guillaume de Villehardouin built an impregnable fortification, walling the eastern slope to enclose an area large enough to accommodate a great cathedral and many houses below the camp.

From the top of the fortifications, two views, one of the austere black mountains rumbling with thunder to the west, one of the broad sunny valley to the east, afforded a contrast that has a parallel in the difference between the preconception that most people bring to this area, and what they find there.

Crossroads of the Crusaders

What every schoolboy knows about Sparta is that its men were the self-denying, self-disciplined soldiers of a barracks state, asking nothing more than is stated in Simonides' epitaph for the three hundred who, hopelessly outnumbered, died with their leader Leonidas, holding back the Persians at the pass of Thermopylae:

> Stranger, bear this message to the Spartans,
> that we lie here obedient to their laws.

The view to the west is toward scenery wholly consistent with such an ideal: there, frugality would be a harsh necessity, climate would train in hardihood. But the valley of the Eurotas, where the Spartans actually lived, is a watered plain, and where there is level land and water to nourish it, Greece blooms. Today, this valley is lush with shade trees, orange and lemon orchards, olive groves, verdant fields. The Mycenaean gold cups found at Vaphio suggest that the earlier inhabitants enjoyed the good life before the Dorian ancestors of the Spartans came, and even after, down into the seventh century B.C., the area had abundant connections with the East. It is true that Sparta did not have the advantages of a port and sea-borne commerce that brought wealth to many other city-states, but neither did it lack local resources. The Spartan life was self-imposed: agriculture, carried on by the helot population, was used to support an army whose only activity was to train itself in the skills of war.

The single-mindedness of the resulting society is shown by the epitaph of a Spartan mother:

> Demaeneta sent eight sons to encounter the phalanx of the foes, and she buried them all beneath one stone. No tear did she shed in her mourning, but said this only: 'Ho! Sparta, I bore these children for thee.'

But Guillaume de Villehardouin did not long enjoy the view from Mistra. He and the King of Sicily made an alliance with the Despot of Epirus to help the Despot march on Thessalonika against the Emperor Michael Paleologue, who had just usurped the throne. On the plain of Pelagonia, Michael's forces defeated them; de Villehardouin was taken prisoner. After three years of captivity, the ransom by which he regained his freedom included ceding to the Emperor the three strongholds of Maina, Monemvasia, and Mistra.

Thenceforth, the area became a despotate ruled by younger members of the Paleologue family; during the two hundred years that the dynasty maintained itself after Michael's recapture of Constantinople in 1261, the area below de Villehardouin's citadel developed into one of the major cities of Greece.

A fourteenth century renaissance in Mistra revived the Greek classics, developed a new generation of Greek philosophers. The names of Pericles and Leonidas were heard again; Plethon proposed reforms for a regenerated Hellas; Bessarion urged that the emperors change their title from King of the Romans to King of the Hellenes.

Art and architecture flourished: the three churches that now remain from many more, the Metropole built early in the fourteenth century, the Peribleptos built a little later, and the Pantanassa of the fifteenth century, display frescoes among the finest in Greece.

Since the despots were the sons or brothers of the emperors, Mistra was the city of the inheritors of empire; the last Byzantine emperor of all, Constantine XIII, was crowned here.

It was he who died in the final attempt to defend the walls of Constantinople in 1453. The Turks had previously gained control of all surrounding areas. Mohammed II completed the great fortress of Roumeli-Hissar above the city on the Bosporus, then closed the vise. In Justinian's church of Hagia Sophia, thenceforth, until our own time, to

be a mosque, he inaugurated the Turkish rule that gripped Greece for the next five hundred years.

Today, the Mistra of the Crusaders and the Mistra of the Byzantines are both ghost cities, but in the convent of the Pantanassa, eight nuns live on among the ghosts. The abbess comes from a family of journalists, one of whom died in the Greek resistance during World War II. She has relatives in the States; I asked if she would like me to bring them a picture.

She stood before the tan-washed wall of the convent, beside a brilliant bougainvillea vine in bloom. Her habit was black as a Greek shadow; her hands were covered by its folds. Her white face and large dark eyes were emphasized by their frame of black veiling. Her head inclined slightly to the left. As I prepared my picture, I thought of the frescoes on the Pantanassa walls.

Mistra is in the middle of the country; the Latin occupiers maintained their footholds longer on the peripheral parts of Greece. Rhodes, the easternmost Aegean island which looks straight into Asia Minor, has suffered foreign suzerainty over much of its history; in our own day, the Italians held it to the end of World War II.

In the classical period, Sparta and Athens both exercised periods of control; so did the Persians and the Macedonians. But after the death of Alexander, the island achieved an independence that lasted into Roman times. This was the period of its apogee. Its position made it the entrepôt of trade both with the Levant and with Alexandria, where amphorae have been found that contained the Rhodian wine exchanged for Egyptian wheat, their handles marked with the Sun God and the Rose of Rhodes. Its schools of philosophy were such that the young men of Rome—Cicero, Caesar, Augustus, Tiberius—finished their education with a grand tour to Rhodes. Rome adopted the Rhodian maritime code intact. The island's sculpture included the Laocoön and the

105-foot bronze Colossus named among the Seven Wonders of the World.

Rhodes was Apollo's personal property: Pindar's seventh Olympian ode explains the island's origin and also that of the three cities other than the capital which still adorn its coast:

"... The ancient legends of men
tell how, when Zeus and the immortals divided the earth
Rhodes had not yet shone in the sea's water,
but the island was hidden in the salt depths.

Helios was gone, and none showed forth his lot.
They left him with no guerdon of land,
that blameless god.
He spoke, and Zeus would cast again, but Helios would not
    suffer it, for he said
under the gray sea he had spied, as a growth from the floor,
a land to foster multitudes, kindly to sheep.

Straightway he bade Lachesis of the golden veil
lift up her hands, nor deny
the gods' great oath
but assent with the son of Kronos, bending her head; the
    island rising thereafter
into the bright air should be his. The words' end was
    accomplished
with a true fall. Out of the winding water the island

blossomed, held of the father of searing sun-rays
master of horses that breathe fire. Rhodes mixed with him
    bore
seven sons, that displayed the shrewdest wits of the men of
    old time.

Of these, one sired Kamiros,
Ialysos, eldest born, and Lindos; sundered, they held
the land of their patrimony in triple division,
each a city, and these are called by their names. . . ."

But the island's independence ended in the second century A.D. when Rhodes was brought within the Roman imperial administration. In 656 it was captured by the Saracens and during the Byzantine Empire it was sporadically harried by them and by the Seljuks of Haroun al Rashid. The Saracens sold the fragments of the Colossus, which had been toppled by an earthquake, to a mainland junk dealer who, according to legend, found himself possessed of nine hundred and eighty camel-loads.

After the beginning of the Crusades, the island was held by a succession of Western adventurers, sometimes acknowledging allegiance to the Byzantine Emperor, sometimes practicing independent piracy, often treating their fief as a staging area for campaigns against the Asia Minor mainland.

When the tide of events turned against the West in the thirteenth century, one of the groups to be expelled from the mainland was the Knights of St. John of Jerusalem. Between 1271 and 1291, Bibars, Sultan of Egypt, and his three successors took both the Krak des Chevaliers, the immense fortress which the Knights had built on the mainland opposite Cyprus, and St. John of Acre; with the Kingdom of Jerusalem at an end, the Order withdrew. First it went to Cyprus; then in 1306 it bought the island of Rhodes from the Genoese admiral who governed it in the name of the Emperor.

For over two hundred years the Knights held their new outpost; even after the capture of Constantinople, when the newly installed Turkish sultans sent expeditions to reduce this bastion of the West, they withstood two sieges, in the second of which Suleiman I is said to have lost ninety thousand men. The Knights recognized the implications of these attacks, however, and the permanence of the loss of the Holy Places; in 1522 they arranged a capitulation and withdrew to their final island, Malta.

Crossroads of the Crusaders

The Rhodes of today looks not unlike the Rhodes of their era. The Knights were also called the Knights Hospitallers; their Order was instituted in the eleventh century to give aid to pilgrims on the Crusades; their Great Hostel at Acre accommodated a thousand wayfarers. The Order comprised knights, clerics, serving brothers; the Knights' civil habit was black, their battle dress red, with a square white cross on the chest.

A porthole's-eye view of the harbor and town as the greatest of the Grand Masters of the order, de Lastic and d'Aubusson, successively built and fortified it, shows a medieval masterpiece: crenelated walls pierced by powerful gates protect the inner hill with the Hospital—now a museum of rare quality, the series of "Inns of the Tongues" where knights from the various countries of Western Europe could dine with others speaking their language, and, at the top, the Church of St. John and the Castello—the Palace of the Grand Master.

Ashore, as one mounts, controversy over the desirability of restoration does likewise. Through the centuries, a number of the buildings of the Knights fell into ruin; just over a hundred years ago, the Church of St. John and the Palace of the Grand Master were destroyed by earthquake and explosion. Their recent rebuilding is the more vividly argued because of the unpopularity of the personality who sponsored it, Mussolini.

The anti-restorationists like their antiques genuine, abhor synthetic patina and alabaster elevators, intersperse their aspersions in regard to the Castello with references to Hollywood.

The pro-restorationists note that nevertheless minute specifications were available: the profile of the street is now as it used to be. When hard pressed, they retire to the sea, inviting the antis either to join them on a boat in the harbor, or just to look upward from the long jetty where three brown-sailed windmills grind meal in preserved picturesqueness.

CHAPTER 15 *The Monasteries*
of the Meteora

THE word "monastic" comes from the Greek *monos*—alone. But St. Basil, who was born in Caesarea in Asia Minor just at the time that the Emperor Constantine adopted Christianity and moved the capital of the empire to the east, early turned the monasticism of Greek Orthodoxy away from the hermetical form initiated by St. Anthony in the Egyptian desert, and into a communal asceticism.

Hermits and anchorites continued to live to themselves alone—St. Simeon Stylites is said to have spent thirty years atop a 60-foot pillar—but they were very few in comparison with the large numbers of men

218

and women who undertook a life of contemplation away from the world in the monastic communities of Byzantine times.

As the lines of empire began to be broken, and successive incursions of barbarians ravaged Greece, the locations of the monasteries which had been established in inaccessible places to enable their occupants to be alone in spiritual contemplation also offered secular refuge.

Northern Greece provided two fantastic sites for such withdrawal. One was the isolated eastern tip of the Chalcidic peninsula, ending in the 6500-foot peak of Mount Athos. The other was the group of curious rock formations, the Meteora of northwest Thessaly.

Mount Athos is said to have been chosen originally for solitary living by Peter the Anchorite; Athanasius the Anchorite, a friend of the Emperor Nicephorus Phocas, grouped various hermits into little communities here and in A.D. 963 founded the monastery of Grand Lavra, regarded as the most beautiful on the peninsula today. From then until the period of foundations ended in A.D. 1545, numbers mounted; grouped in twenty monasteries, nearly five thousand persons live on Mount Athos now.

Visits to these monasteries are limited to males. In A.D. 1060, access to the mount was forbidden "to any woman, to any female, to any child, to any eunuch, to any smooth visage"; while this rule has been rescinded and reimposed on various occasions down the centuries, it is now in force.

The construction of the monasteries typically takes the form of a high-walled hollow square, with the church in the middle, the cells of the monks along the walls, a refectory, and a belfry.

For a long time, particularly because the monks promptly established good relations with the sultans after the Turkish conquest, the early mosaics, the wealth of frescoes—some by the Macedonian school of the fourteenth century, more by the Cretan school of the sixteenth century, the painted and enameled ikons, and the vast collection of priceless

manuscripts remained intact. In the revolutionary waves of the nineteenth century, however, loss and damage, particularly to the manuscripts, was very considerable.

Since the 1920's, Athos has been a theocratic republic, recognized by
the Greek constitution; a Greek governor represents the state there, but
administration is in charge of a Holy Community of one representative
from each monastery.

At the monasteries of the Meteora, visitors of both sexes are received
and may spend the night. The road from the east edges back up the
gorges cut by the Peneus River as it crosses Thessaly to the Thermaic
Gulf until the stark wall of the Pindus Range looms against the western
sky.

Approached in the dark, on a night of rain, as the headlights of the
bus sweep with the last turns of the ascent, the effect is as though one
had entered a mountain cavern; the Meteora look like colossal stalag-
mites, rising toward a ceiling made indeterminate by hanging cloud.

They are gray vertical columns of sandstone, left by prehistoric erosion like the stones of the Giant's Causeway in Ireland or the buttes of
the American Southwest, but so smoothed by the action of those long-
vanished waters, so regular, so slender in circumference, and so high,
they look not like natural phenomena but like unexplained artifacts.

The monastic communities that in the troubled thirteenth century
first set themselves to fast and pray on the tops of these extraordinary
columns were alone indeed—they were rather like corporate St. Simeons.

Access, until very recent times, was in rope slings winched up by cable
on hand-operated windlasses through a free fall of several hundred feet,
or by jointed ladders of 70 to 130 feet in length, which could be pulled
up in time of danger. At the Metamorphosis the rope sling is still the
means by which provisions and supplies—sand and cement, when I was
there—are hoisted.

People can now enter on foot. The bus stops at the end of the road

on the other side of the rock ravine; by daylight, the iron-nerved driver chivvies it around in a space between sheer rise and sheer drop until it heads the other way. Some twenty of us got out in the drizzling dark; two lanterns cast flat pools of rain-flecked light on the ground as we prepared to walk the rest of the way.

Shallow depressions in the rock offer foot space. "Take it slowly," said one of the men with lanterns—it was obvious that here one would not make the same mistake twice. Foot by carefully placed foot, we reached the bottom of the ravine.

On the far side, cement steps have been laid, and there is even a guard wall next to the precipice. For the rest of the arrival, all that is needed is a sound pair of lungs and a stout heart.

Rooms, with water laid on, and a refectory for visitors have been added to this cliff top. The family that takes care of them includes a fine, sturdy girl, Baia, who draws water for their own use from a well—amazing that the interior of this stone cylinder should contain a well—as it has been drawn for five hundred years, except that her vessel is a jerry-can.

First, she supplies the fifteenth century circular stone kitchen, where the family's cook pots are placed over a fire made in the center of the floor. This interior is very like a small Treasury of Atreus: the beautifully beveled blocks of the stone ceiling are laid in a cone like the top of a beehive, with an exit hole at the apex to let out the smoke; their contours are so well designed that at least on a day of quiet air the draft pulls well enough to leave the room clear of all except the nostalgic smell of wood fires laid over generations.

The permanent population of the Meteora monasteries is dwindling to the vanishing point. There were once as many as twenty-four of these establishments; four—Great Meteora, Barlaam, Hagios Stephanos, and the Metamorphosis—are now inhabited. At Roussani, one nun lives alone on her pinnacle.

The Monasteries of the Meteora

At the Metamorphosis, where there are cells for fifty, the precarious clinging to life of a monk thought to be over a hundred years old brings the present total to three. One of the others keeps very much to himself; the third shows visitors the church with its finely carved ikonostasis.

He also illustrates the means of summoning the monks to their offices. In the covered way which passes the church door and leads to the refectory, a slab of pine hangs suspended by a wire fastened at its balanced center. Some 3 inches thick, 16 broad, and 6 feet long, the corners rounded, it has the patina of great age and much handling.

Near one end, a smooth-worn hole perforates it, holding a small wooden hammer shaped like a capital gamma.

The monk removes the hammer, beats an announcement on the wood. It is a wordless but entirely intelligible recitative, a succession of long notes, short notes, changes of pitch and timbre. He taps a sharp emphasis at the end of the slab; then, after a running sequence of short strokes, applied as he moves, another more muffled emphasis near the center; then back and forth until his message has been conveyed. It is the monastic equivalent of military bugles, African drums.

In the morning, the whole bizarre landscape can be seen from a point at the edge of the monastery grounds. Off to the left is the monastery of Hagios Stephanos, whose column is now connected with the massif by a gangway across the crevasse. To the right, uninhabited columns lead away toward Roussani, the place of the solitary nun. Across, in a high cave formation like those of Mesa Verde in the States, a pair of vultures ogle; shortly, they slide off their ledge, wings set in immobile glides, banking with the currents over column and chasm and rivered plain.

Below is the crevasse down and up which we climbed the night before; the opposite rock face shows traces of alternative trails, some that have eroded out, the one in use now. And there where the road terminates is the bus, ready to start down the mountain and climb again over the still higher ridges to the west.

CHAPTER 16

Borderland of Epirus

FROM the tall, black, fir forests at the crest of
the Pindus range, where a 5,500-foot pass is the gateway for east-west
traffic across northern Greece, the military road, potted with chock holes,
hairpins down into Epirus.

This wild, northwest region on the Adriatic just below Albania has a
history at once separate from and linked with that of the rest of
Greece; it is the area where the Turkish influence remains most identifiable today.

In prehistory, the west coast was one avenue of Dorian in-migration;
its early kings ruled an area which comprised parts of contemporary
Albania. Dodona is here, site of the classical oracle, outranked only by
Delphi, where the will of Zeus was interpreted from the murmurings of
the wind in a sacred oak.

Borderland of Epirus

But Epirus was and remains a part of the Balkans.

In the classical period, it stayed in the shallows of the stream of Greek history. After the Macedonian conquest, it achieved prominence because Philip's wife, Olympias, the mother of Alexander the Great, was an Epirote. In Roman times, there were important relations between the two coasts of the Adriatic.

But when the seat of empire moved east, Epirus again became a marginal area.

It was a separatist region, with periods of independence in the Byzantine era; it became a separatist region again in the late eighteenth century under the Turks, when Ali Pasha of Tepelen in Albania, who started his personal empire as Pasha of Trikkala in Thessaly, shifted his base to the Epirote lakeside capital at Jannina. He gradually amassed control of part of Albania and most of Greece except Thrace and the area around Athens. Under his rule, Jannina grew into a city of some twenty-five thousand, a center of learning where the court, rivaling those of Egypt and Constantinople, received ministers from the Great Powers. Minarets of mosques pricking the skyline, streets of bazaars, imposing houses with rooftops occasionally adorned by storks' nests, and a Turkish bath still show the city as it was in 1807 when Byron visited it and in *Childe Harold* described how

> He passed the sacred Haram's silent tower,
> And underneath the wide o'erarching gate
> Survey'd the dwelling of this chief of power,
> Where all around proclaim'd his high estate.
> Amidst no common pomp the despot sate,
> While busy preparation shook the court,
> Slaves, eunuchs, soldiers, guests, and santons wait;
> Within, a palace, and without, a fort:
> Here men of every clime appear to make resort.

225

The place which Ali Pasha occupies in Greek history is a dual one. Politically, his quasi-independence improved Greek chances of throwing off the Turkish yoke; when the Sublime Porte declared him to be in rebellion in 1820, he intrigued with the Greek revolutionaries for support. But the sultan's forces closed in on him, bottling up his troops in Jannina. On the night of February 22, 1822, after taking refuge with his wife and a small guard in one of the monasteries on a fishermen's island in the lake, he was surprised and murdered. His head was thereafter exposed as a warning against civil disobedience not only in Jannina but in Constantinople.

As he died, he gave instructions that his wife should be killed to prevent her falling into the hands of his enemies. The Greek population of the city, hearing of this precaution, understood why it was on his mind. Some fifteen years earlier, Ali's son, Mouktar, had made a conquest of Kyra Phrossini, wife of a Greek merchant of Jannina whose business frequently took him out of town. Like son, like father; Ali's eye wandered in the same direction, but without success. Piqued, the Pasha ordered the lady and her suite of sixteen attendants taken to the lake and drowned. The Greeks made mournful poems about it.

But it is outside the capital that the life of Epirus can best be seen, unemphasized and undisturbed. About halfway, both in mileage and in vertical distance, between the pass and Jannina, slightly south of the military road, is the little town of Metsova.

The place has its distinctions; it has for centuries been the home of the Averoff family, whose heritage of government service includes that of the present Foreign Minister. Their house, which can be visited, exhibits the details of the traditional domestic life of a wealthy family.

Against a sharp hillside, the lowest floor includes the laundry and buttery on one side, a tack room for many finely caparisoned horses on the other. The entrance floor has a stair well stacked with arms, reception and dining rooms.

Borderland of Epirus

The next floor displays the usual family living quarters, the summer bedroom with windows, the windowless winter room with fur covers on the wall-corner beds, and a low Turkish table before a raised tile stove—all facilities are available within one warmed space. In another room on this floor, armoires contain costumes of fabulous silks, worn through the centuries, and full-skirted, tight-bodiced white greatcoats of sheepskin to protect both men and women traveling in winter by horse or sleigh.

The top floor is the salon, for the reception of distinguished guests— today, the foreign minister's car, with state visitors from other countries, often whirls up to show this vivid record of tradition. Collections of *objets d'art* line these upper rooms, among them the special silver server in which sweetmeats were offered to guests on their arrival by the eldest daughter of the household. The collection of ikons includes a painting that may be an early work by the Cretan Domenico Theotocopulos, later known in Spain as El Greco.

The everyday life of the town centers in a little square near the church under the shade of a spreading oak tree and near a fountain which retains the form of the fountains of classical Greece.

Everyone wears homespun. The ankle-length dresses of the women and little girls, with aprons over them, are colored in soft wines, dull cobalts, browns. Almost without exception, the matrons walking in the streets or chatting at street-side doorways twirl, with the deft automatic gestures of second nature, sticks that twist into thread the fluffs of white wool held in their other hand. The local cottage weaving industry prospers.

On a bench near the big tree, the village elders gather; they wear black caps, white blouses, black baggy knee-trousers, woollen leg-bindings wound like puttees instead of stockings; the black shoes of some of them bear black pompons on the toes. A number hold shepherd's crooks.

Borderland of Epirus

And then there are the children.

Six weeks before I reached Metsova, two of us had spent half a day in the room of the Breughels in Vienna's Künsthistorisches Museum. We had enjoyed them in the large, as color and design. We had enjoyed them in the small, finding more and ever more of the details that lead to the close-in finger-pointing that is futilely combated by exasperated and protective guards.

We had discussed at length the difficulties of Breughel's children: they are not children at all, but grown people drawn littler; their profiles are flat planes with no depth; they have one feature only, their ferrety little eyes. In short, we said, unlike his grown people, his animals, his landscapes, his children are unreal.

Sitting in Metsova, with three of them on my lap, accurate to the last detail, I laughed aloud.

CHAPTER 17 *Island Idyl*

THE fierce local loyalties which made Greek classical history a tale of armed rivalry between city-state and city-state seem to rub off readily on the modern tourist; when Greek visitor meets Greek visitor on their return, conversation is likely to become a hot and possessive exchange of appreciation of favorite areas, vouchsafed antiphonally and uninterruptible in its early stages. By the time the company is exhausted, only the itinerary of Odysseus covers more mileage over the wine-dark sea.

This possessiveness is strongest when the conversation turns to favorite islands, especially small ones.

There is justice in the charge that travelers who skip over the Adriatic islands in their haste to reach the Aegean miss more than they realize.

The Greek royal family summers at Corfu, where abundant fresh water nourishes a flower-filled brilliance. Visitors who have seen this landscape charge others who have not with negligence.

Equally partisan are those who prefer the islands of the Saronic Gulf that ring the easternmost promontory of the Peloponnese: Hydra and Spetsai were the homes of great shipbuilding and shipowning families at the same time that Salem, New Bedford, and Newburyport grew with the prosperity of the masters of the Yankee Clippers. During the Greek War of Independence, these families stripped themselves down to the last sail to finance liberation; when the new government was set up, the two islands were given extra representation in parliament in recognition of their sacrifices.

The cleanliness of these—and indeed of most other islands—is proverbial; their rainwashed brown rocks slope steeply to the sea, ornamented with little harbor towns whose houses are whitewashed outside, pin-neat inside. All over Greece, little donkeys run everybody's errands; on Hydra, the passion for cleanliness is so great that those going up and down the narrow passages between the houses wear pantalettes.

As an afterthought to the Saronic islands, at the end of a day spent seeing Epidauros, Mycenae, Tiryns, and Argos, the island-minded who are also forehanded with reservations can even spend the night in spine-prickled luxury on Bourtzi. This is a fortress-islet in the Bay of Nauplia rather like Chillon in Switzerland, where the castle built by the Venetians, later a home for retired executioners, is now a very good hotel.

The Northern Sporades lie off the eastern mainland, below the Mount Athos promontory. Among them is Skyros, where the twentieth century poet-counterpart of Byron, Rupert Brooke, who died in the ill-fated Dardanelles expedition of 1914, is buried.

Exceptional among the central Aegean Cyclades is Santorin, with its smoking volcano and its surrounding islets which over the centuries have risen from, and disappeared into, the sea.

Island Idyl

Another famous Cycladic island is Tenos, whose port is jammed in mid-August with pilgrimages pouring out of arriving boats and starting the climb to the shrine where a miracle-performing ikon of the Virgin

is believed to be the work of St. Luke; thousands upon thousands of people come every year to camp in the open air and attend the services of the Feast of the Assumption.

East of the Cyclades and south of Lesbos and Chios are the Southern Sporades and the Dodecanese; far north of them, close to the Dardanelles, is Samothrace. To the south, Crete is so large an island that partisans claim recognition for it as a sixth continent.

And so it goes.

As for me, let the ship stop inside the double breakwater of Mykonos, while passengers of all ages, from infants to crones, debark with the agility of porpoises into the caiques clustered at the foot of the overside gangway.

Everyone on shore hurries to the harbor when a boat is in, and since outbound steamers from the Peiraeus reach Mykonos in the late evening, the crowded esplanade and lighted cafés give the town the air of a Verdi opera with full chorus onstage.

Most of the houses of Mykonos are tiny, though a few magnificent buildings, several hundred years old, are maintained by families whose names are known throughout Greece—that of the Campanis family bears three cartouches with initials and dates, showing the descent of the house when it has passed through a married daughter.

But usually a house consists of a few rooms, divided between getting a living and living a life. There is normally a room with a door on the level of the stone walkways—except for the waterside roads where the cross-island bus and the handful of private cars and taxis run, the passages are too narrow to be called streets. Here is kept the family donkey and his food supply of dried seaweed, or the merchandise that the family sells, or the looms for the handweaving of the Mykonian specialties that are sold in Athens as well as in shops around the harbor.

An outdoor stairway often leads to the second floor, where the balcony may be roofed and shaded by a well-trained grapevine, or bright with pots of thyme and flowers; from the balcony one enters the living rooms. Little shops—the bakery, the oil merchant's (when Aristophanes had his fun with the oil-can, he was using a utensil with which everyone is familiar), the fish market, the grocery—are scattered along the passages near the harbor; higher up, a small square with trees opens out at the public wells.

Special lodgings exist in this artist's paradise where painters accredited by the Beaux Arts in Athens may live free of charge. The oldest and their favorite section of the town, called "little Venice" because its second-floor balconies overhang the water, dates from the sixteenth century; the windmills on the hill, with separate sails on each vane, compete with "little Venice" for the artists' preference.

Interspersed among the houses around the harbor are many tiny private chapels, frequently surmounted by little belfries with bell ropes carefully lashed in sailor's knots to forestall ringing by the ceaseless wind. There are some four hundred of these in all, ranging from sanctuaries where the ikonostasis exhibits beautiful Italian carving of the sixteenth century and the lamps are of silver, to buildings in which multiple doors allow tiny spaces to each of several poorer families.

The chapels are both sanctuaries and mortuaries. When a person dies, his remains are placed in a burial ground outside the town. They stay there for three years. Then they are brought back for reinterment in the family chapel.

Some of the larger buildings on the island date from the exile, in the latter part of the eighteenth century, of one of Catherine the Great's discarded lovers whom she made consul at Mykonos with a document that also warned he should return to Russia only if she personally signed a *laissez-passer*. Count de Voinovitz spent some years on the island, constructing for his business office the only tile-roofed building, which now serves as the mayoralty and public library, with other miscellaneous uses. He started an irrigated garden at the other side of the

harbor, where his well with stone water-channels still irrigates the hibiscus, oleander, and other shrubs that now surround the Leto Hotel, and the bougainvillea vine which frames the harbor view at breakfast and dinner on the balcony.

Mykonos gains current prominence from an epic, yet to reach its final episodes, with which even the busy citizens of Athens are familiar in detail: the story of Petros the Pelican, the occasion of a second Trojan War.

Just as Homeric versions differ, there are variants of the Petros epic, but as the Mykonians tell it, three years ago, at the time of the annual migration from Egypt to the Caucasus, a mother pelican was overcome with immediate necessities on approaching Mykonos. Putting together a makeshift nest, she laid three eggs.

At once the news circulated among the harbor houses, and when the eggs hatched, all Mykonos was prepared for foster parenthood. Unable to face so much attention, one chick promptly died. A second succumbed to a surfeit of figs, offered by the islanders. But the third was incurably robust; he lived to become Petros.

Down by the water front, one of the seamen became his special patron; like the cats of colonial New England, he has a flap-door from the seaman's home which permits him to go down to the sea for a morning bath at a time of his choosing. Later in the day, he makes the rounds of the water-front cafés, standing gravely and politely beside the open-air tables, waiting for tossed fish-heads. If a kitten contests his catch, he picks her up by the nape of the neck and dangles her out of the way; his pinch is considerable, and young children are constantly warned against it.

But a year ago last spring, one fine morning, Petros spread his wings and flew away.

The event in itself was sad enough, but shortly an ugly rumor floated back across the wine-dark sea. Petros was said to be on the island of

Tenos, nine sea miles away. Furthermore, he was said to be retained there against his will.

Then started the second Trojan War. Every caique in Mykonos set out for Tenos, the patron seaman in the lead. They anchored in a semicircle, bottling the harbor so that no boat with clandestine cargo might depart.

A delegation visited the police of Tenos with the ultimatum—Petros or else.

The police were placatory. They said that if the Mykonians would return to their ships, and that if the rest of the day passed without incident, under cover of darkness, in the historic Trojan fashion, something might be done.

In fact, at about nine-thirty, with no fanfare, they thought Petros could be returned.

He was.

At eleven-thirty, the victorious Mykonian fleet rounded the entrance breakwater to its home harbor, shouting paeans and beating upon pans.

Promptly thereafter, Petros was formally declared to be a citizen of Mykonos, provided with an identity disc, and clipped of wing sufficiently to prevent flight, though not enough to impair the usefulness of his wings as sails when on windy days he rides the waves in and out among the boats in the harbor.

Today he walks the jetties as an official greeter and poses for picture postcards, a personage whom everyone knows.

In fact, he may even be a political power. There are those who whisper that the defeat of the mayor who had served thirty-eight years, and the installation of Demetrius Passaliades, which occurred at the first election after Petros became a citizen, was due to the pelican vote.

Perhaps, when all is said and done, it is for idyls like this, as much as for the great sites of antiquity, that more and more people come annually to the isles of Greece. There is an immemorial quality to the scene

Island Idyl

when fishermen, seated on the flat stones of a harbor esplanade, mend their nets with intense faces, large needles, and meshes kept taut by the insertion of one big toe, and to the designs, like waves caught in sudden stillness, made by nets drying in the sun; and the visitors from the gray and harried wastes of the North Atlantic appreciate it.

APPENDICES

Acknowledgments

I was going to Greece; I looked for a book that would prepare me for arrival.

Physical descriptions of the chief sites—Delphi, Delos, Olympia, Mycenae, Crete—that I, or any traveller, would be sure to visit interested me only mildly; I could look at these for myself. My concern was for an account—it should be quick and not dead—of the human institutions that caused the sites to come into being and made them what they were in their great days.

Since in my workaday life I am a reporter, I had a preference for the first-hand story, for direct quotes taken from eyewitnesses or near contemporaries—singers of epics and odes, playwrights, poets, historians, philosophers, and more pedestrian recorders in script or stone.

At the same time, I wanted to learn as much as a non-specialist outsider can briefly absorb about the archaeological finds that have made the last hundred years in Greece a succession of discovery and re-covery, of unearthing both the expected and the unexpected.

I didn't find such a book, so after I came back I took a stab at writing one.

The following pages list my formal acknowledgments in recognition of the photographers, authors, translators on whose works I have drawn to illustrate and illumine the experience that awaits the traveller in Greece, where Zeus himself has always been the friend of strangers.

Beyond these are some acknowledgments that are personal.

First in time is my debt to a great teacher. I belonged in another field, but I had one course with Rhys Carpenter, then of Bryn Mawr, later head of the American School of Classical Studies in Athens. It was not only unforgettable—all these years I have remembered it.

The second debt is to coincidence. If the Central Committee of the World Council of Churches had not held its 1959 session on the island of Rhodes, I would not have travelled in Greece that summer, and Francis Pickens Miller and I would not have shared the days that remained after his attendance at this meeting was over.

Nor would I have renewed a friendship dormant since college days with Dorothy Burr Thompson, archaeologist of the Agora, who has since read my manuscript, named it, pointed out pitfalls, introduced me to some recent translations, and opened the way to photographs that are among the freshest here reproduced.

Likewise by coincidence, along highways and seaways, varied new acquaintance came from chance meetings.

There was Helly Couloura—subsequently, when I asked a Greek general if he knew her, his reply was, "Madame, all Greece knows Mme. Couloura," and I felt rather as if I had inquired of a Frenchman whether he had happened to hear of a woman called Jeanne d'Arc.

There was Doula Mourikis, staffer at the Archaeological Museum in Athens, who later checked data for me.

Acknowledgments

There were John and Sophie Halikiopoulos at the Leto Hotel in Mykonos, whose equanimity permitted them, on a morning when the cat had her kittens in conspicuous travail and certain guests were clamorously cross because the inter-island steamer schedule was interrupted, to send the barman to our balcony breakfast table bearing a blushing peach of Olympian proportions, which he placed before Francis with a magnificent gesture and the information, "la poitrine d'Aphrodite."

There was the intrepid Mario, whose bus-driving is gay of manner but iron—accurately-tooled iron—of nerve.

And there was the young girl whose letter is quoted at the end of Chapter 13.

In respect to translations, I made two decisions for personal reasons that went beyond the text. I used the Jowett translation of Plato, and the Gilbert Murray translation of the *Medea,* partly as a link with that other time of intense intellectual excitement when I was a student at Oxford; and the latter also because of a remembered contralto cadence in which I used to hear the *Sons of Erechtheus* chorus sung.

Likewise, I have given the Pericles funeral oration as the late Sir Alfred Zimmern gave it in his *Greek Commonwealth,* because in a workers' education class I once taught the background of democracy from that book to a group of garment workers engaged in a long and bitter strike, and they found it pertinent.

A problem which afflicts any writer on Greece is that of the spelling of proper names. I have made a serious effort to keep my text consistent, while leaving inviolate the texts of the writers whom I quote, but I have abandoned purity in favor of familiar usage in the case of a few individuals—Aegeus among heroes, Cimon, Themistocles and Pericles among men.

One final acknowledgment: my mistakes, and my ignorance, are my own.

PICTURE CREDITS

Picture Credits

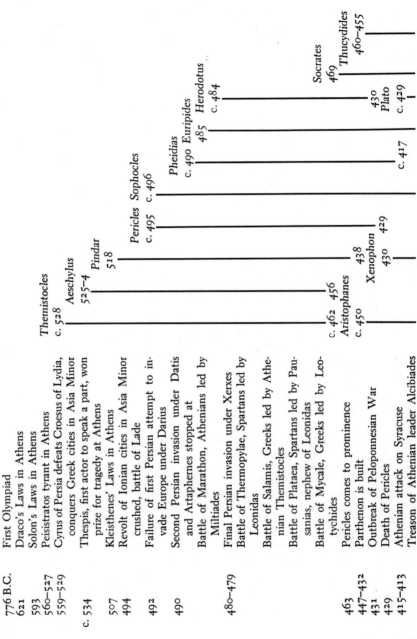

776 B.C. First Olympiad
621 Draco's Laws in Athens
593 Solon's Laws in Athens
560–527 Peisistratos tyrant in Athens
559–529 Cyrus of Persia defeats Croesus of Lydia, conquers Greek cities in Asia Minor
c. 534 Thespis, first actor to speak a part, won prize for tragedy at Athens
507 Kleisthenes' Laws in Athens
494 Revolt of Ionian cities in Asia Minor crushed, battle of Lade
492 Failure of first Persian attempt to invade Europe under Darius
490 Second Persian invasion under Datis and Artaphernes stopped at Battle of Marathon, Athenians led by Miltiades
480–479 Final Persian invasion under Xerxes
Battle of Thermopylae, Spartans led by Leonidas
Battle of Salamis, Greeks led by Athenian Themistocles
Battle of Plataea, Spartans led by Pausanias, nephew of Leonidas
Battle of Mycale, Greeks led by Leotychides
463 Pericles comes to prominence
447–432 Parthenon is built
431 Outbreak of Peloponnesian War
429 Death of Pericles
415–413 Athenian attack on Syracuse
Treason of Athenian leader Alcibiades

Demosthenes 384–322

Praxiteles fl. 364–330

Aristotle 384–322

405	Sparta defeats Athens, Battle of Aegospotami
404	Athens surrenders to Sparta
399	Death of Socrates
371	Thebes defeats Sparta, Battle of Leuctra
362	Epaminondas of Thebes killed at battle of Mantinea
338	Philip II, king of Macedon 359–336, conquers Greece
	Battle of Chaironeia
336–323	Alexander the Great, king of Macedon, defeats Persia, carries Greek culture into Asia
218	Clash of Rome and Macedonia
168	Rome defeats Macedonia, Battle of Pydna
146	Greece becomes a Roman province after revolt is crushed
86	Sulla in Athens
50–53 A.D.	St. Paul visits Greece
67–66	Nero visits Greece
129	Hadrian dedicates Olympeion in Athens
330	Constantinople becomes capital of Eastern Empire
393	Theodosius I stops Olympic Games
529	Justinian, emperor of the East 527–565, closes philosophic schools in Athens
532–537	Justinian builds Santa Sophia
1084	First Crusade
1204	Fourth Crusade
1456	Turkish conquest of Greece
1821–1832	Greek Wars of Liberation

BIBLIOGRAPHY

1. Flying travellers look for substance without weight; the following books, as of 1960, were available either as paperbacks or in compact editions:

   A. ORIGINAL SOURCES

   Auden, W. H., ed., *THE PORTABLE GREEK READER* (Viking)

   Baldry, H. C., *GREEK LITERATURE FOR THE MODERN READER* (Cambridge University Press)

   Crawley, Richard, trans., Thucydides, *THE PELOPONNESIAN WAR* (Everyman)

   Grene, David, and Lattimore, Richmond, eds., *GREEK TRAGEDIES* (Beacon)

   Lattimore, Richmond, trans., *GREEK LYRICS* (University of Chicago)

   Lucas, F. L., *GREEK POETRY FOR EVERYMAN* (Beacon)

   Oates, Whitney J., and O'Neill, Eugene, Jr., eds., *SEVEN FAMOUS GREEK PLAYS*: Aeschylus, *Agamemnon*, *Prometheus Bound*; Sophocles, *Oedipus the King*, *Antigone*; Euripides, *Medea*, *Alcestis*; Aristophanes, *The Frogs* (Everyman)

   Rieu, E. V., trans., Homer, *THE ILIAD*: Homer, *THE ODYSSEY* (Penguin)

   Rose, H. J., ed., *HANDBOOK OF GREEK LITERATURE* (Everyman)

   B. ABOUT GREECE

   American School of Classical Studies at Athens (American address, care of Institute for Advanced Study, Princeton, New Jersey): *GUIDE TO THE ATHENIAN AGORA* New edition forthcoming); *PICTURE BOOK SERIES*: The Athenian Citizen, the Stoa of Attalos, pottery, sculpture, etc. ($0.50 each, postpaid); *GUIDE TO ANCIENT CORINTH* ($0.75, postpaid); *RESTORATIONS OF CLASSICAL BUILDINGS* ($1.10, postpaid)

   Bowra, C. M., *THE GREEK EXPERIENCE* (New American Library)

   Craven, Thomas, *POCKET BOOK OF GREEK ART* (Pocket Books)

   Graves, Robert, *MYTHS, I & II* (Penguin)

   Hamilton, Edith, *THE GREEK WAY TO CIVILIZATION* (New American Library)

   Kitto, H. D., *THE GREEKS* (Penguin)

   Lawrence, A. W., *GREEK ARCHITECTURE* (Penguin)

   Rice, David Talbot, *BYZANTINE ART* (Penguin)

   Robinson, C. E., *HELLAS, A SHORT HISTORY OF ANCIENT GREECE* (Beacon)

   Rose, H. J., ed., *HANDBOOK OF GREEK MYTHS* (Everyman)

   Seltman, Charles, *A BOOK OF GREEK COINS* (Penguin)

   Warner, Rex, *THE GREEK PHILOSOPHERS* (New American Library)

   Zimmern, Alfred, *THE GREEK COMMONWEALTH* (Modern Library)

2. Books not available in paper editions can however be taken before or after one's actual voyage; the following round out the list above:

   Carpenter, Rhys, *GREEK SCULPTURE* (University of Chicago)

   Cottrell, Leonard, *THE BULL OF MINOS* (Rinehart)

Bibliography

Diehl, Charles, BYZANTIUM: GREATNESS AND DECLINE (Rutgers University Press)

Durrell, Lawrence, REFLECTIONS ON A MARINE VENUS (Faber & Faber) (Rhodes)

ibid., PROSPERO'S CAVE (Corfu)

Frazer, Sir James G., GRAECIA ANTIQUA: MAPS AND PLANS TO ILLUS-TRATE PAUSANIAS'S DESCRIPTION OF GREECE

ibid., trans., Pausanias, DESCRIPTION OF GREECE (Macmilan)

Higham, T. F., and Bowra, C. M., eds., THE OXFORD BOOK OF GREEK VERSE IN TRANSLATION (Oxford)

Jowett, B., trans., THE REPUBLIC OF PLATO (2 vols.); THE FOUR SOCRATIC DIALOGUES OF PLATO; Aristotle's POLITICS (Oxford)

Lancaster, Osbert, CLASSICAL LANDSCAPE WITH FIGURES (Dufour)

Lane, Arthur, GREEK POTTERY (Van Nostrand)

Lattimore, Richmond, trans., THE ODES OF PINDAR (University of Chicago)

Liddell, Robert, THE MOREA (Jonathan Cape)

Oates, Whitney, J., ed., THE COMPLETE GREEK DRAMA; all the extant tragedies of Aeschylus, Sophocles and Euripides, and the comedies of Aristophanes and Menander, in a variety of translations (Random)

Pendleton, J. D. S., A HANDBOOK OF THE PALACE OF MINOS (Dufour)

Quennell, M. and C. H. C., EVERYDAY THINGS IN ANCIENT GREECE (Putnam)

Richter, G. M. A., A HANDBOOK OF GREEK ART (Phaidon)

Robertson, Martin, GREEK PAINTING (Skira)

Robinson, C. O., SELECTIONS FROM GREEK AND ROMAN HISTORIANS (Rinehart)

Roux, Jeanne et Georges, GREECE trans. by Lionel and Miriam Kochan (Essential Books)

3. Picture books both foretell and recall; they are widely available in Greece, Western Europe, and the United States; in making a choice, one needs a check book more than a check list.

4. Among regular guide-books, the traveller does well to consider Hachette's GUIDE BLEU, available in English as well as French.